Gift Wraps

Gift Wraps

Lorraine Bodger

A Jane Ross Associates Book

The Stonesong Press, Inc.
Bedford Hills, New York

Book design and illustrations by Lorraine Bodger
Cover design by Liz Trovato
Cover photographs by Fred Slavin

FIRST EDITION

85 86 87 88 89 10 9 8 7 6 5 4 3 2 1

Contents

Introduction

Gift wrapping is a very special craft because, like icing on a cake, it makes a good thing better. *Gift Wraps* is your easy-to-follow guide to everything you need to know to make terrific gift wraps right from the start.

Chapter 1 is a complete, concise rundown of the supplies you will need for gift wrapping. You have many choices and they are all described here. There is a special Shopper's Guide to help you locate the right store for buying each item. Chapter 2 covers basic how-to information about color, wrapping, tying, making bows and attaching gift cards and tags. The instructions and drawings are straightforward and clear.

Chapter 3 tells you how to make your own materials in order to individualize your gift wraps and also save money. You'll find do-it-yourself papers, ribbons, braids, tassels and pompons, fabric bags, tags and cards. Even a novice can do these crafts—no expert skills needed. Chapter 4 gives you a bonus: fourteen pretty patterns (hearts, teddy bear, gingerbread boy and girl, etc.) plus instructions for transferring them out of the book and ideas for using the patterns in your gift wraps.

Chapter 5 is a treasury of fifty different gift wraps for holidays, birthdays, special events and family occasions. There are wraps for different shapes and sizes of boxes, tins, envelopes and sacks, wraps for babies and children, for moms and dads, for newlyweds and golden anniversaries. Copy them straight from the book or use them as inspiration for inventing your own new designs. Chapter 6 is the problem-solving section: a collection of wrapping ideas for sports equipment, checks and theater tickets, enormous presents in huge boxes, enormous presents with no boxes and those perennial gift wrap problems, food and wine.

Everyone gives gifts and almost everyone has to wrap them, too. The gift is an important message—and so is your custom-made wrapping. It's a tangible expression of your feelings, a demonstration of your wish to please and honor the recipient, whether the recipient is your grandmother or your boss or your best friend. So make a little effort and *Gift Wraps* will get you big, big results.

Lorraine Bodger

CHAPTER I
What's Available: a Survey of Gift Wrap Materials

This is a guide to gift wrap materials available in stores and around your own home. Some of these materials are ones you are accustomed to using—standard gift wrap paper, ribbon, gift tags. Some may be materials you have never before thought of using. Keep your mind open to the possibilities. Also remember that although a well-stocked card store or party supply shop is undoubtedly the best all-purpose source of supplies, there are treasures to be found in the stationery store, art supply store and even the notions store.

Boxes

Almost any gift looks better in a box. It is certainly easier to wrap when it's boxed, so make a point of saving good cardboard boxes all year round. They can be fitted inside each other so they won't take up too much houseroom if you assign them one shelf in a closet. Dress and coat boxes, shoe boxes, appliance boxes, housewares boxes, boxes from gifts you receive, little jewelry boxes—save them all and half your gift wrapping problems are solved. With any luck, you'll have the right size and shape when you need it.

Of course, sooner or later you will have to go scouting for a big, sturdy carton to package some large gift. By now you probably know the merchants in your town with the best box supplies—the liquor store, supermarket or greengrocer. You'll want boxes that are clean, with the tops still attached and all the sides and corners intact.

Most party supply stores and five-and-tens carry a good stock of gift boxes in a variety of sizes. Buying a box adds to the cost of your gift, but (depending on the gift) you may feel it is a worthwhile investment. Choose a box in which the gift fits comfortably, neither too snugly nor too loosely.

Party supply stores and card shops also carry a variety of die-cut boxes that you assemble yourself. They come in several shapes, sizes and colors: large and small cubes, octagonal boxes and boxes that look like take-out food cartons. There are often special Christmas boxes, too, with embossed or printed scenes and Victorian motifs. Many of the mail order catalogues offer very pretty nested round, square or octagonal boxes in bright, shiny colors and patterns. Import stores are also a good source for these nested boxes. And don't overlook a cake-decorating supply store for cake boxes or small boxes with cellophane windows, millinery supply house for hat boxes, copy shop for manu-script boxes and even the post office for mailing tubes.

Papers

You can indulge in all kinds of interesting and exceptional papers for gift wrapping (Japanese rice paper, fine artist's papers, marbleized bookbinding papers), but let's be reasonable instead. Most of the time you will want to wrap gifts with standard papers that are easy to get, easy to use and moderately priced.

Standard gift wraps in rolls or folded sheets are the papers you will choose time and again. They come in dozens of colors, prints and stripes and there are new patterns every season. You can find matte, glossy and high-gloss surfaces. There are special papers for every occasion and papers suitable for any occasion. Metallic papers come in smooth gold, silver and colors and in several embossed textures. Metallic and high-gloss papers are coated papers, i.e., the color is applied in a thin film to one side of the paper. They are not receptive to being folded and refolded; the color tends to flake off at the folds and they begin to look messy and shopworn. Work carefully with them and try not to wrap and rewrap.

Tissue paper is essential for lining or padding your gift box, and it's very attractive for wrapping the box, too. It comes in white, pastels and brilliant colors, often with an assortment of colors in the same package. It is so thin that it tears easily, but its thinness also makes it useful for wrapping around odd shapes. You can see through it, so use several sheets at once or use it only for wrapping clean, unprinted boxes.

Inexpensive solid-color papers are wonderful to use for making your own patterned paper (see Chapter 3) or when you have many gifts to wrap at one time. These papers include brown kraft paper (available at a card shop, five-and-ten or stationery store), 18" × 24" pads of bond and newsprint paper (art supply store), shelf paper (five-and-ten or housewares store) and economy-size rolls of gift wrap (card shop or discount store).

Hand-me-down papers are the ones you rescue from the floor when someone is unwrapping birthday presents (or Christmas presents or shower gifts). Save any sizable undamaged pieces of good-looking patterns and colors and iron them on a very low dry setting to get out the wrinkles before using them again. Cut out clean, unwrinkled smaller pieces to use for wrapping small gifts.

Many other papers have limited uses in gift wrapping.

● Construction paper: too brittle for wrapping packages but very useful for making gift tags and package appliqués

● Origami paper: comes in brilliant colors, wonderful for cut-paper decorations on gift tags and cards

● Unlined index cards: available in white and several pastels, the best choice for making simple gift tags (see Chapter 3)

● Cellophane: fun to use for wrapping food

● Crepe paper streamers: narrow rolls of crepe paper, used for wrapping some large gifts

● Newspapers, maps and posters: good for wrapping packages

Ribbons and other ties

Standard gift wrap ribbon, like standard gift wrap, is terrific stuff. It's reasonably priced, widely available and easy to use. It comes in many, many colors, a number of patterns and several textures and widths. There are even special seasonal designs. It is undoubtedly the ribbon you will want to use most often. Look for the following kinds:

● Satin sheen ribbon: ¾ inch wide or wider, sometimes labeled "sticks to itself when moistened"; the all-purpose ribbon

● Curling ribbon: narrow width, ridged, can be curled over a scissors blade

● Florist's ribbon: acetate satin, very crisp, in a variety of widths up to 5 inches

● Craft ribbon: feels a bit like starched thin cotton, comes in calicos and other patterns and holiday designs

● Metallic ribbon: silver and gold, comes wound on a cardboard spool

Avoid imitation velvet and taffeta ribbons as they are very poor quality and will cheapen your gift wrapping.

Apparel ribbon is a great treat to use on a special gift. Depending on which width and pattern you choose, the ribbon can be prohibitively expensive if you have dozens of packages to wrap. But for a very important present, for a single bow or for only one gift (for example, a friend's birthday present), it helps to make a memorable wrapping.

Apparel ribbon comes in many widths, from ⅛ inch to 3 inches, many fashionable colors and some interesting textures. Keep in mind the following ribbon styles and textures: satin; grosgrain; velvet; taffeta; embroidered; gingham; dotted; picot-edged; plaid; metallic; striped.

Yarns from the five-and-ten or yarn store are excellent gift ties, especially when you use several strands at once—perhaps several different colors of worsted weight or bulky yarn. You can buy small skeins of knitting or crewel yarn in several colors and keep them on hand for wrapping purposes, because the price is right. There's no need to buy the bulky yarns packaged especially for gift wrapping.

Other needlework materials are also suitable for gift wrapping: crochet cottons; threads like Speed-Cro-Sheen; metallic yarns; rug yarn; ombre or tweed yarn; heavy embroidery cottons; macramé cords and rat tail. Save up odd bits left over from needlework projects and stash them with your gift wrapping supplies.

Stretch ties are elasticized cords, often metallic, which are not tied like ribbon but simply stretched from corner to corner or around a package.

Here are some suggestions to inspire you when you want to use a tie other than satin sheen gift wrap ribbon.

● Christmas: gold or silver ribbon; red and green plaid taffeta ribbon; red and green yarn; red or green gingham ribbon

● Casual and sporty: striped grosgrain ribbon; cotton string; crochet cotton; shoelaces; mailing cord

● Playful and childlike: fat yarns; curling ribbon; jumbo rickrack; ribbon printed with children's motifs

● Warm and homey: dotted grosgrain ribbon; flat eyelet; several strands of yarn; gingham ribbon

● Craftsy: jute; macramé cord; rug yarn; soutache braid; embroidered ribbon

● Elegant and tailored: stretch ties; grosgrain ribbon in neutral colors; velvet tubing; gold or silver cord

● Opulent and luxurious: wide flat lace; picot-edge satin or taffeta ribbon; several strands of double-face satin ribbon; velvet ribbon

Cards, tags, labels, stickers and specialty items

These are the finishing touches for your wrapped gift: cards, tags or labels for writing the name of the recipient, a short message and your own name; stickers and specialty items for trimming the package.

Ready-made folded gift cards (with matching envelopes) or tags are convenient to use and often quite well-designed. (Turn to Chapter 3 if you would like to make your own tags and cards from scratch.)

Thin cardboard tags generally used for mailing or merchandising have string loops that can be slipped onto the ribbon after knotting but before tying the bow. Write your message on one side and decorate the reverse, if you like, with a sticker, appliqué or stamped design.

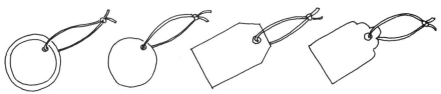

Self-adhesive and gummed labels can be attached directly to the package. You can put two labels together back to back, punch a hole in one corner, add a string loop and attach to the ribbon as described above. You might even write a message on a small label and press the label over the center of the bow, or put back-to-back labels on the ends of the bow.

Self-adhesive decorative seals and stickers are now available in strips, sheets and booklets. They come in designs for every taste, from superheroes to hearts and flowers. Use them to perk up a package, ribbon or gift tag.

Self-adhesive commercial seals and stickers can be used as decorations. There are squares and rectangles of all sizes for you to play with as well as dots from ½ inch to 1¼ inches in diameter in bright blue, orange, green and yellow. You might wrap a package in shiny red paper, polka-dot it in neon yellow and tie it with fat yellow yarn.

Gummed stickers and seals include the familiar gold-, silver- and metallic-colored stars as well as three sizes of notarial seals in red, blue and gold. Gummed stickers will not adhere to gloss-finish papers; use them only on matte-finish gift wraps, kraft paper, shelf paper or tissue paper.

Special materials that you can apply directly to a wrapping are tucked away in the party supply store, card shop and craft supply store.

● Glitter pens: draw directly on the paper wrapping, making squiggles, dots, stars or printed messages

● Sequins and spangles: adhere with white or clear glue in patterns or try spelling out a name or date

● Self-adhesive letters or numbers: spell out a name or announce a birthday or anniversary

● Doilies: use doilies whole or cut out motifs or borders to glue to the package

● Pompons from ball fringe: use instead of bows

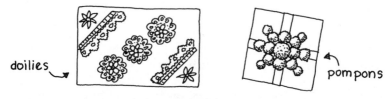

doilies

pompons

Small novelty items add an extra finishing touch to a wrapped and tied present. These items need not be large or important; they are attached to amuse and make the gift wrap more interesting. Depending on the item, you may tie it to the ribbon after knotting but before making a bow; you may attach it with a bit of very thin wire twisted around the bow; you may secure it with tape loops.

For Christmas, add a few small shiny balls, a sprig of artificial holly, a jingle bell or a candy cane. For other occasions, add some pretty artificial flowers or fruits, a tiny gold or silver basket, plastic charms (the kind used for party favors), a paper parasol, a few balloons, curly paper streamers, a miniature art print or postcard.

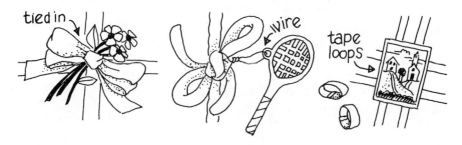

tied in

wire

tape loops

Interesting containers

There are many containers other than boxes that you can use when you are packaging a gift. Some are almost as all-purpose as a cardboard box: baskets, shopping bags, paper sacks, plastic boxes and tote bags. If you do it with imagination, you can pack a book, a batch of cookies or a pair of pajamas in any of these.

Jars, tins, envelopes and even small buckets are in the in-between category: They can be used for many different gifts but not all gifts. An unexpected combination using one of these containers can be amusing—how about a bright red round tin packed full of rolled-up argyle socks? On the other hand, picture a setting of flatware rattling around in a jar—it's all wrong. Choose carefully what gifts you put in these containers.

Other interesting containers include small zipper cases, cardboard tubes, lingerie cases, tiny matchboxes, plastic eggs, plastic or wood berry baskets, metal recipe boxes, large or small portfolios, Shaker-style wood boxes, planters, desk organizers and child-sized suitcases.

If you are planning to use an interesting container, it's important to match the gift to the container or vice versa; very often these unusual containers are best suited to specific categories or gifts. For example, almost any real kitchen container (baking pan, loaf pan, casserole) had better be packed with something in the food line or it will seem slightly odd and inappropriate. Or, to put it the other way around, don't pack a new camera in a flower pot. You'll strike a much better note if you put it in a canvas shoulder bag with a few rolls of film tucked in, too. And you might very well give a gardener two or three new tools, a new pair of gardening gloves and a variety of seeds packed in cellophane grass in a clay flower pot tied with grass green ribbon.

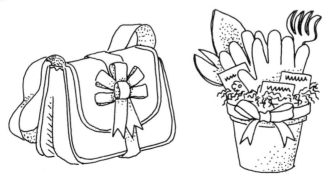

Sometimes the container is an integral and very welcome part of the gift. Here are some gift-plus-container ideas you might like to try:

● Cosmetics carry-all filled with skin-care goodies

● Small travel case stuffed with sample sizes of shampoo, soap, toothpaste, etc.

● College book bag holding a variety of paperbacks

● Vinyl-coated wire desk basket packed with office supplies like typing paper, pens, paper clips, etc.

● Plastic refrigerator box of homemade snacks or nuts

● Ceramic cookie jar filled with homemade cookies

● Child-size overnight case loaded with puzzles, games and small toys

● Small backpack filled with baby-care supplies and a few infant toys

● Lacy lingerie case with six pairs of pantyhose inside

When you are wrapping an interesting container there are three possible approaches:

● If the container is an easily wrapped shape, you can simply place the gift in the container (lining first with tissue paper if necessary) and wrap as usual with paper and ribbon, checking Chapter 2 for wrapping techniques.

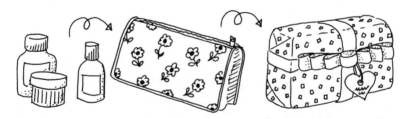

● You can place the gift in the container and wrap it only with ribbon and a little something extra—a pretty gift tag, some artificial flowers, a sprig of holly.

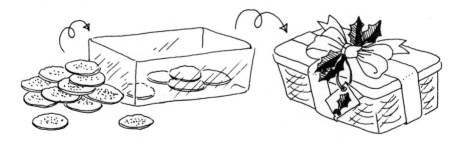

● Or you can wrap the gift first, place it in the container (lining or cushioning if necessary) and add a bow or some other trimming.

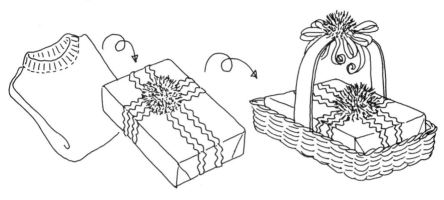

Shopper's guide

For a generally good selection of gift wrap papers and ribbons first try the five-and-ten, card shop, party supply store and stationery store. In addition, each of these stores and many other kinds of stores have special items (mentioned in this and other chapters) that will enhance your wrappings. The following alphabetical guide will help you find what you need.

Apparel ribbon: fabric store; notions store; five-and-ten; millinery supply store
Appliqués: notions store; five-and-ten; fabric store
Baskets: import store; five-and-ten; department store
Baskets (miniature): party supply store; craft supply store
Baskets (mushroom, grape, berry): supermarket; greengrocer
Bond and newsprint paper: art supply store, craft supply store
Boxes: party supply store; card shop; five-and-ten; department store; cake decorating supply store; millinery supply store
Buckets (cardboard): paint store
Buckets (metal): hardware store
Buckets (plastic): housewares store; five-and-ten
Cellophane: party supply store; craft supply store; card shop
Charms and other favors: party supply store; card shop; five-and-ten; cake decorating supply store
Construction paper: five-and-ten; art supply store, craft supply store
Craft ribbon: craft supply store; party supply store; card shop
Crochet threads: yarn or needlework shop; five-and-ten; department store
Doilies (paper): party supply store; housewares store; five-and-ten

Eggs (plastic): craft supply store

Embroidery and crewel yarns: yarn or needlework shop; notions store; five-and-ten; department store

Envelopes: stationery store; card shop; five-and-ten

Florist's ribbon: florists' supply store; craft supply store; party supply store

Flowers (artificial): millinery supply store; five-and-ten; craft supply store; florists' supply store; notions store

Fruits (artificial): florists' supply store; party supply store

Garlands (paper or metallic): party supply store; Christmas supply store or Christmas department; five-and-ten

Gift cards: card shop; party supply store

Glitter pens: craft supply store; party supply store; five-and-ten

Index cards: stationery store; five-and-ten

Jars (canning, for food gifts): hardware or general store; five-and-ten

Jute: craft supply store

Kraft paper: stationery store; card shop; five-and-ten

Labels: stationery store; party supply store; five-and-ten

Macramé cords: craft supply store; needlework shop

Origami paper: import store; craft supply store; party supply store

Paper sacks (brown): supermarket; delicatessen; liquor store

Paper sacks (shiny, colored): party supply store; card shop

Parasols (paper, miniature): party supply store; card shop; import store

Plastic boxes and containers: housewares store; hardware store; five-and-ten; stationery store; plastics supply store

Postcards and miniature prints: museums; craft supply store; card shop

Recipe boxes: five-and-ten; stationery store

Self-adhesive letters and numbers: stationery store; hardware store; art supply store

Sequins and spangles: craft supply store; notions store; five-and-ten

Shelf paper (regular and self-adhesive): housewares store; five-and-ten

Stickers and seals: stationery store; card shop; party supply store; five-and-ten

Streamers (crepe paper): party supply store; five-and-ten; craft supply store

Streamers (curly paper): party supply store: five-and-ten

String and mailing cord: stationery store; five-and-ten; hardware store

Tags: stationery store; card shop; party supply store; five-and-ten

Tins: kitchen or baking supply store; import store; five-and-ten; party supply store

Tissue paper: five-and-ten; card shop; art supply store; craft supply store; party supply store

Trims (rickrack, braid, ball fringe, etc.): fabric store; notions store; five-and-ten; craft supply store; department store

Velvet tubing: fabric store; notions store

Wire (thin): craft supply store; florists' supply store; hardware store

Wooden boxes (Shaker-style): craft supply store

Yarn: yarn or needlework store; five-and-ten; department store

CHAPTER 2
Wrapping Basics

In this chapter I will explain the Mystery of the Perfectly Wrapped Gift, answer the Riddle of the Eight Great Ribbon Bows and reveal other Deep Dark Secrets closely guarded by experienced gift wrappers. You, too, can learn the basic wrapping skills, and in fact, you'll find there's very little mystery at all. You will want to refer to the how-tos in this chapter both when a project in the book requires a particular technique and when you need a quick brush-up before carrying out one of your own designs.

Basic choices: colors and patterns

Choosing the colors and patterns for a gift wrap can be a mind-boggling task. You will find it easier and more fun if you think about it as a process similar to putting together an outfit for a special occasion: First you consider the mood and formality of the occasion. Next you decide which basic dress or suit to wear. Finally, you add accessories that match or contrast.

A gift wrap design requires the same kind of basic planning. First consider the occasion: Is it a child's birthday? An engagement shower? A country Christmas? Then decide on a basic paper in an appropriate color or pattern. Next, pick a ribbon or tie to match or contrast with the paper and, finally, choose any little extras to dress up the wrapping. Here are some examples to give you a start.

● Christmas: shiny green paper; red and green plaid ribbon; red gift tag; bright yellow star stickers applied to the paper

● Adult birthday: blue and silver striped paper; silver cord; silver gift tag

● Child's birthday: paper printed in pink, turquoise, yellow and orange; bright pink ribbon, yellow balloons for trimming

● Baby shower: pale blue and white plaid paper; blue and white ribbons; tiny pale yellow stuffed duck for trimming

● Graduation: gray paper; maroon ribbon; navy blue and maroon gift tag and trimmings

● Housewarming: quilt-patterned paper in light brown, rust and moss green; moss green ribbon and gift tag; rust and brown dried flowers tied into the bow

● Adult birthday: white paper printed with lavender flowers; lavender and pale green ribbons; violet gift tag

● Teenager's birthday: yellow paper with red polka dots; red ribbon with white dots; red and white striped gift tag

● Easter: paper patterned in peach, yellow, lavender and apple green; apple green gingham ribbon; gold foil-wrapped chocolate bunny for trimming

● Golden wedding anniversary: white paper with embossed pattern; gold ribbons; gold gift tag

● Valentine's Day: red paper printed with white hearts; white satin ribbons; red silk roses tied into the bow

Basic equipment

Aside from paper and ribbon, all you need for basic gift wrapping is a pair of scissors, a tape measure, a glue stick and a dispenser of transparent tape. It's that simple. Adding a ruler, a small pointed scissors, a roll of double-face tape (sticky on both sides), a container of white glue plus a round artist's brush for applying the glue makes it possible to do even more than basic wrapping. Some special projects require special materials and equipment; you will find these listed at the beginning of each project.

How to wrap a box with rectangular ends

1. Determine the correct size of the piece of wrapping paper as follows: Measure around the box with a tape measure. Add 3 inches to the measurement. That will be the length of the paper.

Measure the box as shown in the drawing, from arrow to arrow. That will be the width of the paper.

2. Unroll or unfold the paper and cut it to the correct size. If you are cutting out a large piece of paper, you may find this method helpful: Measure the paper and notch the edges to mark the length and width. Place the paper along the edge of a table with a square corner, with the width-marker notch at the very edge of the table as shown. Crease the paper along the edge of the table. Cut across the paper on the crease. Put the excess paper aside.

Now turn the paper and place it with the length-marker notch at the edge of the table. Crease the paper along the edge of the table. Cut the paper on the crease. Save the small excess piece for wrapping a small gift.

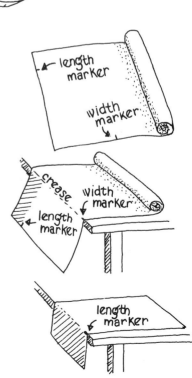

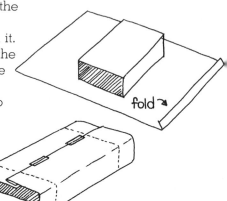

3. Fold under one short edge of the paper about 1 inch. Turn the paper wrong side up and center the box on it. Bring the ends of the paper up over the box very snugly, with the folded edge on top. Tape the paper at the center. The folded edge should be parallel to the sides of the box.

fold

4. Complete one end of the box at a time: Fold the paper down, making creases at the top edge, inner corners and sides as shown by the heavy lines in the drawing.

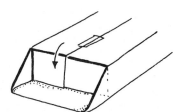

5. Fold the sides toward the center and crease the sides and flap as shown.

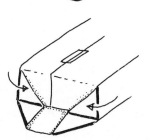

6. Fold the remaining flap up, crease the bottom edge and tape the top edge with one long piece of tape. (This is neater than putting two or three small bits of tape.)

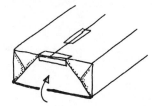

7. Repeat this process on the other end of the box. Turn the box over so that the right side is up.

right side up

How to wrap a box with square ends

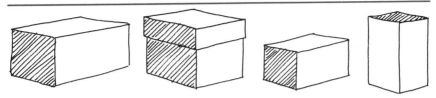

1. Cut the paper to the correct size as follows: Measure around the box with a tape measure. Add 3 inches to the measurement. That will be the length of the paper.

Measure the box as shown in the drawing, from arrow to arrow, beginning and ending the measurement about ½ inch below the middle of each side. That will be the width of the paper.

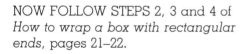

NOW FOLLOW STEPS 2, 3 and 4 of *How to wrap a box with rectangular ends*, pages 21–22.

5. Fold the sides toward the center and crease only at the side edges.

6. Fold the remaining flap up, creasing the bottom edge and the two diagonals. Fasten at the center with a piece of tape.

7. Repeat this process on the other end of the box. Turn the box over so the right side is up.

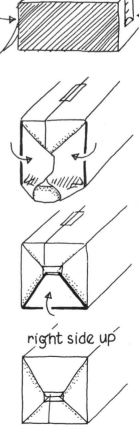

right side up

How to wrap a cylinder

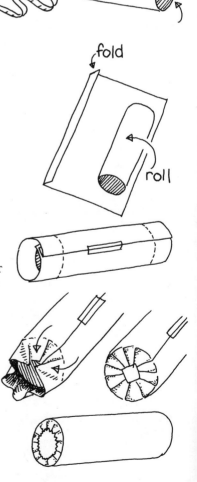

1. Determine the correct size of the piece of wrapping paper as follows: Measure around the cylinder with a tape measure. Add 2 inches to the measurement. That will be the length of the paper.

Measure the cylinder from arrow to arrow as shown, beginning and ending the measurement about ½ inch below the center points of the ends of the cylinder. That will be the width of the paper.

2. Unroll or unfold the paper and cut it to the correct size. If you are cutting out a large piece of paper, use the method described in step 2 of *How to wrap a box with rectangular ends*, page 21.

3. Fold under one long edge of the paper about 1 inch. Turn the paper wrong side up and center the cylinder at the opposite edge of the paper. Roll the cylinder in the paper and tape the folded edge.

4. Complete one end of the cylinder at a time: Fold the paper down to cover the end in small, evenly spaced pleats as shown. Tape the pleats closed and cover the tape with a self-adhesive or gummed sticker.

5. Repeat this process on the other end of the cylinder.

How to wrap a large box

If you are giving a very large gift in a box (a refrigerator, for instance), check Chapter 6 for ideas about packaging enormous gifts. If you must wrap a large gift with no box, consider putting it in another kind of container altogether: laundry bag with stenciled or iron-on decorations; duffel bag tied up in ribbons; a great big fabric sack that you make yourself following directions in Chapter 3; large tote bag or even a pretty pillow case tied with ribbon.

But if you want to wrap a large box (a stereo, a model train set, a dollhouse), you will find that the main difficulty is finding a piece of paper both long enough and wide enough to go around the box and cover the ends as well. You can cope with this problem by using one of the techniques described below. Start with an extra-long roll of paper, 30 inches wide and 20 feet long.

● **Technique #1:** If the box is narrower than the roll of paper, measure around the box, add 3 inches to the measurement and cut off a piece of paper as long as the final measurement. Fold under one end of the paper about 1 inch. Turn the paper wrong side up, center the box on the paper and wrap the paper snugly around the box with the folded end on top. Tape the paper in several spots along the folded edge.

Now cover the ends as much as possible, using the technique shown on page 22. Tape the paper securely to the box. Measure the remaining uncovered area of one end, add 2 inches to the length and 2 inches to the width and cut a piece of paper to that measurement. Glue the piece of paper over the end of the box. Repeat for the other uncovered end.

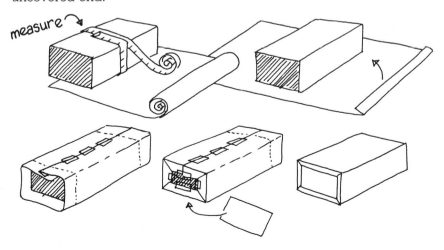

● **Technique #2:** If the box is wider than the paper, it can probably be accommodated by turning it the long way on the paper. To
wrap it this way, measure around the box as shown, add 3 inches to
the measurement and cut off a piece of paper as long as the final
measurement. Fold under one end of the paper about 1 inch. Turn
the paper wrong side up, center the box on the paper and wrap the
paper snugly around the box with the folded end on top. Tape the
paper in several spots along the folded edge.

Now complete the sides using the method shown on page 22 (first
trimming off excess paper if necessary) or the method described above
in Technique #1.

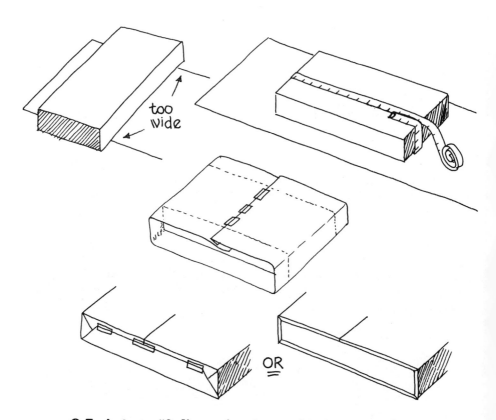

● **Technique #3:** If your box is very big, you can glue together
several pieces of paper to make one sheet large enough to wrap the
box. Use white glue applied sparingly at the very edges of the paper.
Be sure to wipe up any smears and spills. If your paper is patterned
or striped, when piecing it together be careful to keep the stripes and
patterns running in the same direction. You can avoid that problem
entirely by piecing together a pattern and a matching solid color.

密 密 密

How to wrap a small box

The trick when wrapping a small or tiny box (under 3" × 3") is to keep the elements in scale: Don't overwhelm the box with large prints or stripes, wide ribbons or complicated tied-on extras.

Choose a solid-color paper or a paper with a small print or dot. Stripes don't usually work very well unless they are pale in color or very narrow. Make use of scraps of paper you have saved from other packages or try one sheet of bright origami paper, a sheet of pretty stationery, a piece of blue-lined graph paper, colored typing paper or even a section of paper cut from a patterned or shiny paper sack or shopping bag.

Tie the box with curling ribbon or another ¼-inch-wide ribbon, ⅛-inch-wide satin or grosgrain apparel ribbon, thin cord or string, crochet cotton, crewel yarn or embroidery thread. Make the bow neat and small, cutting the ends short so they do not overhang the box.

If you want to add a little something to perk up the wrapping, tie on a miniature gift tag (either purchased or homemade; see Chapter 3), one or two small artificial flowers, one little favor like a paper parasol, a dollhouse miniature or a tiny china animal.

If you are giving a tiny gift that has no box or if you would just like to wrap it in a more interesting way, consider these possibilities:

● Make a tiny fabric sack (see Chapter 3) from some appropriate but interesting fabric like brocade, satin, velvet, pinwale corduroy or suede. Tie with a complementary ribbon or cord.

● Wrap the gift in tissue. Place the tissue packet in the center of a lacy or embroidered hanky. Bring the hanky up around the gift and tie with ribbon.

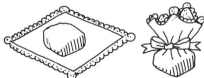

● Find a very special small container for the small gift: an inlaid wood box; handcrafted ceramic crock; antique tin; cut-glass sugar bowl with lid; beaded purse; miniature chest; unusual basket.

How to tie up a gift

There are two basic ways to tie up a gift with ribbon, cord or yarn: on the square and on the diagonal. With either method you can end either by tying a pretty bow or by making a tight knot and snipping off the excess ribbon. If you are planning to attach a lavish bow (see *Eight great ribbon bows*, page 30), make a knot and snip off the ends close to the knot.

Knowing how much ribbon to allow is a matter of experience, so while you are learning use an inexpensive reel of curling ribbon or a small ball of yarn.

On the square

1. Holding a 1-foot-long end of ribbon on top of the box, wrap the long end of ribbon once around the width of the box. Twist the ribbons around each other as shown.

2. Holding the short (1-foot-long) end of ribbon, stretch the long end across the length of the box, under the box, up again on the other side and across the twist. Snip off the long end leaving 1½ feet of ribbon to work with.

3. Slip the long end under the twist as shown. Slip the short end under the ribbon as shown. Pull both ends tight.

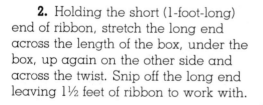

4. Tie the ribbon ends in a knot. If you want to make a bow, do it now, keeping the right side of the ribbon (if there is one) outermost. If you want to end with a knot, tie the ribbon ends together once more and cut off the excess ribbon.

On the diagonal

1. Cut a long piece of ribbon. Find the midpoint and place it near one corner of the box.

2. Take the ends of ribbon down and around the two adjacent corners of the box, keeping the ribbon flat on the sides and back of the box.

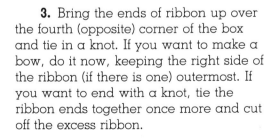

3. Bring the ends of ribbon up over the fourth (opposite) corner of the box and tie in a knot. If you want to make a bow, do it now, keeping the right side of the ribbon (if there is one) outermost. If you want to end with a knot, tie the ribbon ends together once more and cut off the excess ribbon.

Other methods of applying ribbon

1. Tape the ribbon in place: Arrange each piece of ribbon flat on the front of the wrapped box and bring it smoothly around the back of the box. Cut off the excess ribbon. Tape the ribbon ends neatly to the back of the box. The box will look perfect on top and only slightly less than perfect on the back.

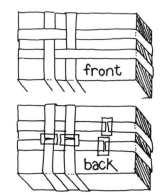

2. Ribbon can be glued to a package. Use glue stick applied sparingly to the back of the ribbon and press ribbon in place on the wrapped box.

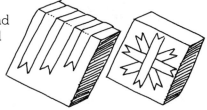

Eight great ribbon bows

These bows are made with ribbon and attached to a wrapped gift. Satin sheen gift wrap ribbon is the usual choice, but you may experiment with florist's ribbon, craft ribbon, metallic ribbon and apparel ribbon. If you use satin sheen ribbon labeled "sticks to itself when moistened," you can construct the bows with no glue at all; simply moisten the ribbon when instructions call for gluing. With any other ribbon, use glue stick for all construction. Curling ribbon, yarns and cords are not appropriate for making these bows.

The size you make the bow depends on the size of your wrapped gift. A large package generally requires a large, lavish bow; a small package looks better with a neat, scaled-down bow. Instructions are given here for medium-size bows; increase or decrease the size according to your needs.

Attach a bow either directly to the package or to the ribbon tied around the package, using tape loops, small pieces of double-face tape or dabs of glue stick or white glue. You can see many examples of attached bows on pages 39–41 and in Chapter 5.

⊞ ⊞ ⊞

Simple Loops Bow

1. To make the basic bow, cut four
pieces of ribbon, each 10 inches long.
Shape one piece into a loop and glue
the ends together, overlapping them
½ inch. Glue the loop together at the
center as shown. Repeat this process
with the other three pieces of ribbon.

2. Glue the loops together as shown
to make the bow.

3. Cut one piece of ribbon 3 inches
long and another 4 inches long. Shape
the 3-inch piece into a loop and glue the
ends together, overlapping them ½
inch. Do the same with the 4-inch piece.
Glue the two loops together as shown
and then glue over the center of the
bow.

Variation #1

This makes a slightly larger and
fancier bow. If you use two colors of
ribbon it is even more impressive.
Make the basic bow as described in
steps 1 and 2 above. Make another
basic bow using pieces of ribbon 13
inches long. Glue the two bows together
at their centers, lining up the loops as
shown. Make the pair of smaller loops
for the center and glue them in place.

Variation #2

This variation has three basic bows
stacked up, topped with a pair of
smaller loops. Make the first basic bow
with four pieces of ribbon each 8 inches
long, the second with pieces 10 inches
long and the third with pieces 12 inches
long. Glue the basic bows together at
their centers. Make the smaller loops
and glue them in place on the bow.

Crisp Full Bow

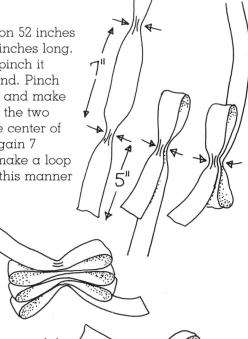

Make this bow with 1¼- to 1½-inch-wide crushable ribbon. Try the softer variety of satin-sheen gift wrap ribbon, craft ribbon, florist's ribbon, single-face satin or taffeta apparel ribbon; very stiff satin-sheen or stiff apparel ribbon like grosgrain or velvet are not suitable. You will also need a 6-inch piece of thin wire.

1. Cut one piece of ribbon 52 inches long and a second piece 12 inches long. Take the longer ribbon and pinch it together 5 inches from one end. Pinch again 7 inches farther along and make a loop pointing up, bringing the two pinches together to make the center of the bow. Pinch the ribbon again 7 inches from the center and make a loop pointing down. Continue in this manner until there are six loops.

2. Wrap the wire tightly around the center two or three times and twist the ends of wire together securely. Clip off the excess wire.

3. Gently crush the 12-inch piece of ribbon at its midpoint and then wrap it twice around the center of the bow, covering the wire. Knot the ends of ribbon together once on the back of the bow. Trim all four ribbon ends in points and twist them to the back of the bow.

Fluffy Bow

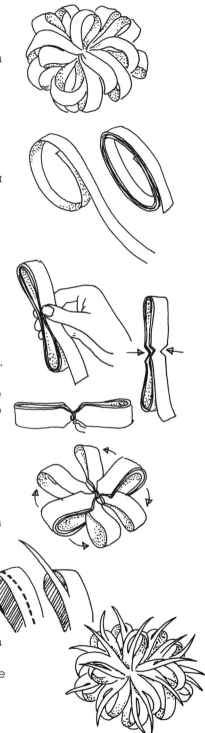

Use ¾-inch-wide satin sheen ribbon and a 6-inch piece of thin wire for this bow.

1. Unwind some ribbon from a reel and measure off 12 inches. Do not cut. Shape the 12-inch piece of ribbon into a ring. Wrap more ribbon smoothly around the ring nine times for a total of ten rings. Now cut the ribbon.

2. Bring opposite points of the ring together and hold them firmly in the center. There should be equal amounts of ribbon on either side of your fingers. With a sharp scissors, snip wedges out of the ribbon, cutting through all layers. Be careful not to cut right through the center. Wrap the wire twice around the center and twist it tightly on the back to secure it. Clip off the excess wire.

3. To fluff out the bow, draw each loop out and twist it up to either the right or left. Begin with the innermost loops and work out. You will have to fiddle with the loops to position them in the most attractive arrangement.

Variation

Clip one edge of each loop as shown to make points that stand up from the loops. Each cut must begin below the center of the loop and widen slightly on the other side. Cut all the points in the same direction, toward the center of the bow.

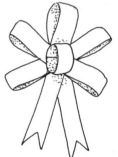

Medallion Bow

Use satin sheen gift wrap ribbon, double-face satin apparel ribbon or grosgrain apparel ribbon for this bow.

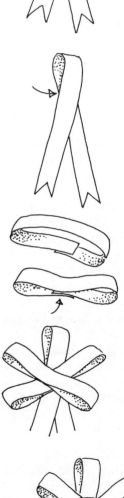

1. Cut one piece of ribbon 12½ inches long. Bend it over as shown and glue at the intersection. Snip the ends in points.

2. Cut two pieces of ribbon, each 10 inches long. Form one piece into a loop and glue the ends together, overlapping them ½ inch. Glue the loop together in the center as shown. Repeat with the second piece of ribbon.

3. Glue the loops over the longer piece of ribbon as shown.

4. Cut one piece of ribbon 4 inches long. Form a loop and glue the ends together, overlapping them ½ inch. Glue the underside of the loop to the medallion as shown.

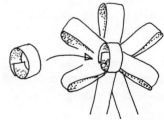

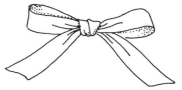

Neat Flat Bow

To make this bow you'll need a piece of apparel, craft or florist's ribbon 1 inch wide and 24 inches long—and a friend willing to hold up two fingers for you to work on. Follow the diagrams carefully step by step.

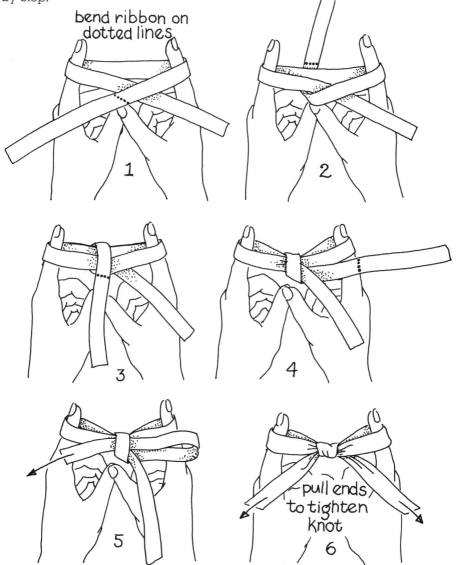

Flat Loops Bow

This bow is made of loops of
graduated sizes. By changing the size
and number of loops or grouping
several bows together, you can make
quite a variety of package ornaments.

1. Cut one piece of ribbon 12½
inches long, another 10½ inches long
and a third 8½ inches long. Shape one
piece into a loop and glue the ends
together, overlapping them ½ inch.
Glue the loop together at the center as
shown. Repeat this process with the
other two pieces of ribbon.

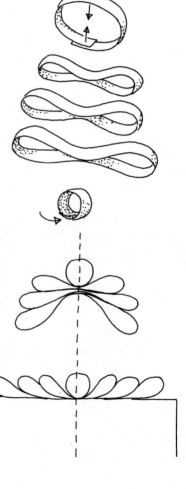

2. Cut one piece of ribbon 4½
inches long. Shape it into a loop and
glue the ends together, overlapping
them ½ inch.

3. Glue the four loops together in a
stack, perfectly centered, as shown. The
bow curves down until you glue or tape
it to the flat surface of the gift box.

Twisted Loops Bow

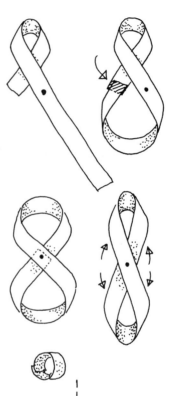

Make this bow with gift wrap ribbon labeled "sticks to itself when moistened."

1. Cut one piece of ribbon 9 inches long, another piece 12 inches long and a third piece 15 inches long. Mark the center of each piece with a tiny pencil dot.

2. Hold the 9-inch piece as shown in the drawing. Twist the lower end and bring it up. Overlap ½ inch, moisten and hold in place until secure. Move the overlap directly under the pencil dot and pivot the ribbon to elongate the loops. Moisten under the center and hold for a moment until secure. Repeat this process with the other two pieces of ribbon.

3. Cut one piece of ribbon 3 inches long and shape it into a round loop. Overlap the ends ¼ inch, moisten and hold until secure.

4. Stack the twisted loops centered on each other. Moisten between the centers and hold in place until secure. Moisten the underside of the round loop and place it in the center of the bow.

The bow curves down until you glue or tape it to the flat surface of the gift box.

Flower Bow

To make the Flower Bow you will need two contrasting colors of ¾- to 1-inch-wide ribbon (Color A for the petals and Color B for the leaves) plus three or four small pompons cut from ball fringe for the center.

1. Using Color A, cut six pieces of ribbon each 4 inches long. To make one petal, bend one piece of ribbon as shown, making a point at the top, and glue at the overlap. Repeat with the remaining five pieces of ribbon. Arrange the petals in a circle with the ends overlapping in the center. Glue together in the center.

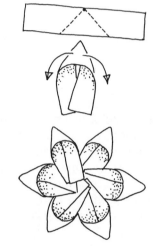

2. Using Color A again, cut six pieces of ribbon each 3 inches long. Repeat the process described above to make a second circle of petals.

3. Glue the two circles of petals together at the center, positioning the smaller petals between the larger ones.

4. Using Color B, cut two pieces of ribbon each 5 inches long. To make the leaves, bend and glue each piece of ribbon as described above. Turn each leaf over and glue underneath the larger circle of petals.

5. Glue three or four pompons in the center of the flower to cover up all the cut ends.

Basic gift wraps with ribbons and bows

There are countless beautiful ways to arrange ribbon and bows on gift wrapped boxes. The following drawings, showing some of the best, most popular designs, will give you ideas and inspiration for your own gift wraps. In all the examples the boxes are first wrapped with pretty paper, then the ribbon is tied or taped in place and finally the bow is made separately and attached to the box.

1. Any of the bows will look perfect on this package, but the Fluffy Bow (page 33) is used most often. The bow can be centered, as shown, or placed slightly off-center.

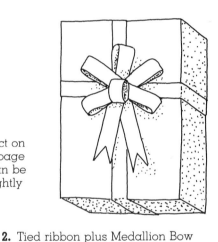

2. Tied ribbon plus Medallion Bow (page 34) placed above the center of the box

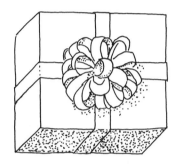

3. Tied ribbon plus Crisp Full Bow (page 32) placed to the right, as shown, or left of center

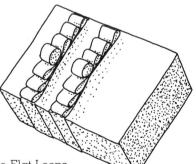

4. Taped ribbon plus two Flat Loops Bows (page 36), one centered and the other left of center

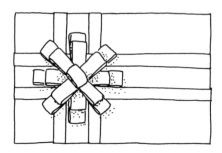

5. Taped ribbons plus Variation #1 of the Simple Loops Bow (page 31). The ribbons and bow can be off-center, as shown, or centered.

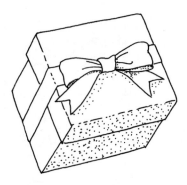

6. Taped ribbon plus a centered Neat Flat Bow (page 35)

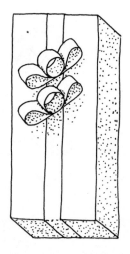

7. Taped ribbon with two small Flat Loops Bows (page 36) placed above the center of the box and slightly on the diagonal

8. Taped ribbon plus Twisted Loops Bow (page 37)

9. Taped ribbon with Variation #2 of the Simple Loops Bow (page 31) placed slightly to the right of center

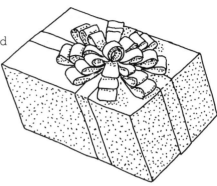

10. Tied or taped ribbon plus Flower Bow (page 38)

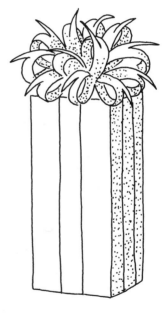

11. Tied ribbon plus clipped variation of the Fluffy Bow (page 33)

12. Taped ribbon plus Simple Loops Bow (page 31) placed a little above the center of the cylinder

How to attach gift cards and tags

A gift card (with matching envelope) is generally larger than a tag, with plenty of room for the name of the recipient, a short message and your own signature; a gift tag has no envelope, may be folded or flat and often has at one end a punched hole with a thin string loop or cord tie. A gift card or tag may be placed in the gift box before wrapping or be attached to the outside as an integral part of the gift wrap design.

There are several ways to attach a card or tag to the outside of a wrapped package.

● Tuck the card or tag under the ribbon or bow. If the gift wrap has a slick surface, you may need a small tape loop on the back of the card or tag to hold it in place.

● Glue the tag (with no string loop) to the gift wrap, positioning it to work with the gift wrap design.

● Tie up a package or sack (paper or fabric) with ribbon, making a knot; slip the string loop of a tag onto the ribbon and tie a bow. Alternatively, slip the string loop onto the ribbon, knot again, clip off the excess ribbon and add a separately made bow.

● Instead of string, thread pretty cord or yarn through the punched hole and tie a tag to the handle of a shopping bag or around the gathered neck of a paper or fabric sack.

● Tape the string loop of a tag directly to the gift, concealing the tape under the bow or under a decorative element.

● Attach the tag or card with a gummed or self-adhesive sticker.

You will find more information in Chapter 2 (purchased cards and tags), Chapter 3 (do-it-yourself cards and tags) and Chapter 5 (gift wrap designs with cards and tags).

CHAPTER 3
Do It Yourself: Making Your Own Materials

In this chapter you will find papers, ribbons, fabric sacks, envelopes, gift cards and tags that you can make very easily; you need only a short amount of time and absolutely no special skills. The raw materials are inexpensive and readily available, some of them right in your own home. Many of the projects are excellent for older children to do alone or for you to do with the younger ones. When you're making do-it-yourself paper, ribbons or tags, try to make a few extra so you'll have them on hand when you need them in a hurry.

Here are some general suggestions for gift wraps using do-it-yourself materials from this chapter:

● Spatter-print paper with matching yarn braid ties and mosaic-design gift card

● Stamped paper with paper ribbon and bow and applied design gift tag

● Painted paper with curling ribbon and a folded gift tag

● Stamped paper with a yarn tie and pompon decoration

● Fabric sack with pinked fabric ribbons and cut-paper-design gift tag

Do-it-yourself papers

Painted paper

You will need: roll of solid-color paper (shelf paper or matte-finish gift wrap) or an 18″ × 24″ pad of bond paper; jars of acrylic tempera paint (white, red, blue, green and yellow); flat and round artist's brushes; paper cups for mixing new colors; containers of water for rinsing brushes

Cover the work surface with newspaper. Shake the jars to blend the paint thoroughly. Spread out the solid-color paper and paint simple designs in a pattern all over the paper. There is no need to plan exactly the placement of the elements, but do try to distribute them evenly over the entire piece of paper. You will find this gets easier as you gain experience. Try some of the following ideas: thick and thin stripes; hearts; stars; simple bows; squiggles; spirals; dots in one, two or many colors; simple flowers; checkerboard squares; dotted lines; geometric shapes; Christmas motifs like candy canes or holly leaves with berries; pumpkins; shamrocks; stick figures.

Here are some general hints on painting and on mixing new colors:

● Remember that red and blue make violet; red and yellow make orange; white added to any color will make a pastel tint of that color.

● To make a new color, pour small amounts of two colors into a paper cup and mix vigorously with a brush. Adjust the color by adding a bit more of one color if necessary.

● Be sure to rinse your brush thoroughly in clean water when you change colors; the colors will get muddy if you don't.

● Don't dilute the paint with water if you can avoid it since water makes the paper wrinkle.

● Allow the paper to dry completely before using it for wrapping.

Spatter-print paper

You will need: roll of solid color paper (shelf paper, kraft paper or matte-finish gift wrap) or an 18″ × 24″ pad of bond paper; jars of acrylic tempera paint; inexpensive paint brush, ½ to ¾ inch wide; disposable containers for mixing the paint with water

Cover the work surface and floor very well with newspapers; the spatters fly all over. Prepare a small pitcher of water for diluting the paint and a container of water for rinsing the brush. Keep a roll of paper towels handy for spills. Shake the jars to blend the paints thoroughly.

Prepare all the colors you will be using. Pour an inch of paint into a disposable container and dilute with water until it reaches the consistency of fruit juice, stirring it with the brush. If you are mixing new colors, be sure to blend the undiluted paints first and then add water to get the right consistency. Rinse your brush in clean water before mixing each new color.

Spread out the solid-color paper. Dip the brush in paint, hold it about a foot above the paper and tap the brush sharply with your other hand. Drops should spatter all over the paper. If they don't, either you did not tap hard enough or there was not enough paint on the brush. Try again and continue spattering until the paper is well covered with dots. Experiment to find out how you like different effects—a thin coverage of tiny dots, lots and lots of large dots, etc. Let the paper dry thoroughly.

Spatters of any of the bright colors are very effective on white or light-color paper and white dots are wonderful on bright or deep colors. Try multicolor dots on white paper, too. If you want to spatter two or more colors, let each color dry before adding the next.

Stamped paper

You will need: roll of solid-color paper (shelf paper, kraft paper or matte-finish gift wrap) or an 18″ × 24″ pad of bond paper; large gum erasers; X-acto knife or other thin-bladed craft knife; ink pads in one or more colors

With a ball-point pen or felt-tip marker, draw a motif on the long or short side of a gum eraser. Color the sections of the eraser that are not part of the motif. Carefully cut them away with the knife, to a depth of ⅛ inch, leaving the motif raised. Press the stamper into the ink pad and practice printing it on scrap paper. Then print either a random or an orderly pattern all over the solid-color paper.

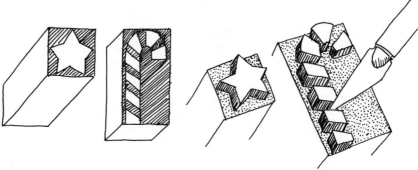

Do not try to cover the entire paper with a solid, stamped design; aim instead for a simple, effective pattern. Any of the motifs shown below can be copied onto an eraser and used in that way. It's a good idea to make several stampers of each motif you are printing; when the edges of one stamper wear away, retire it and take a fresh one.

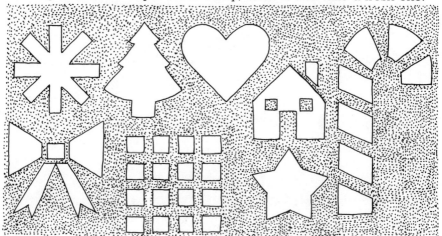

Do-it-yourself ribbons and ties

Paper ribbons

Make paper ribbons by measuring and cutting 1-inch-wide strips of pretty paper. Glue or tape the paper ribbons to a wrapped gift, overlapping and adding new strips when needed. Make the bow separately: Simple Loops Bow (page 31), Medallion Bow (page 34) and Flat Loops Bow (page 36) can all be made with paper ribbons.

● If you use kraft paper or plain white paper for the ribbons, dress up the strips by stamping a design on them before applying them to the gift box. See the stampers on page 46.

● Solid-color paper ribbons are especially pretty when cut with pinking shears.

● Ribbons made with thin paper can be curled over the edge of a scissors blade. Use several curls instead of a bow on top of a gift.

● When making a bow, try a combination of patterned and solid-color papers.

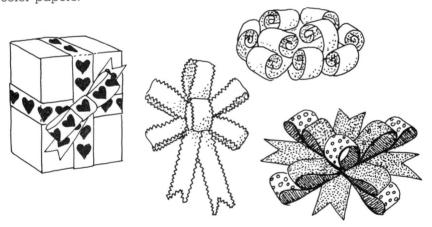

Pinked fabric ribbons

There are two ways to make fabric ribbons:

● If you have some long pieces of cotton or cotton-blend fabric, simply cut 1-inch-wide (or wider) strips with pinking shears. Spray-starch the strips, iron them and store them wrapped smoothly around a cardboard tube. Use the pinked fabric strips in place of ribbon.

● If you have a short length or small piece of fabric, you can make a long, continuous length of ribbon this way: Bring the ends of the piece of fabric together with right sides touching to make a tube. Offset the edges 1 inch or however wide you want the ribbon to be, as shown in the drawing, and pin. Machine-stitch a narrow seam, using a lock stitch if your sewing machine has one; if it doesn't, stitch a second time right over the first line of stitching. Now begin cutting the fabric 1 inch from the edge, making a strip 1-inch wide, snipping through the seam each time it comes around. Cut all the way to the end of the fabric. Wrap the ribbon around a cardboard tube and use as needed.

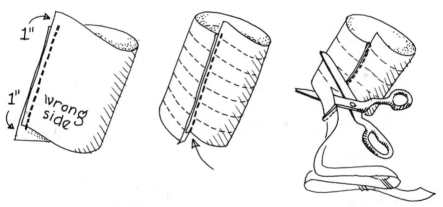

Scrap yarn braids, tassels and pompons

Collect all those little balls of leftover yarn and put them to good use in your gift wraps. Feel free to mix up the colors, textures and weights of yarn when you make braids, tassels and pompons.

To make a braid, use either three strands of fat yarn or three groups of thinner yarns: Cut long pieces of equal length (longer than you actually need—the finished braid will be shorter than the individual strands) and knot the ends together. Braid the strands or the groups just loosely enough so the braid lies flat. Knot the strands or groups together at the end and clip off any excess yarn.

To make a medium-size tassel, wind two strands of 3-ply or 4-ply yarn loosely around a 4-inch piece of cardboard about ten times. Slip an 8-inch piece of yarn under the strands at the top of the cardboard and knot tightly as shown. (At the appropriate time, you can use the ends of the knotted piece of yarn for attaching the tassel to a gift wrap.) Slide the yarn off the cardboard. Wind a piece of yarn a few times around the tassel about three-quarters of an inch from the top and tie tightly. Trim the lower ends of the yarn to the desired length.

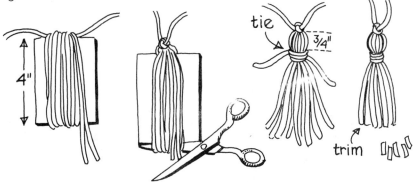

To make a medium-size pompon, cut a piece of shirt cardboard as shown in the drawing, with a hole in the middle. Wind two strands of 4-ply yarn around the center section of the cardboard about 70 times. Slip an 8-inch piece of yarn around the strands through the hole in the middle of the cardboard. Tie tightly. Slide the blade of a scissors under the yarn at the top of the cardboard and snip the yarn. Do the same at the bottom of the cardboard. Fluff out the yarn and trim to a round shape.

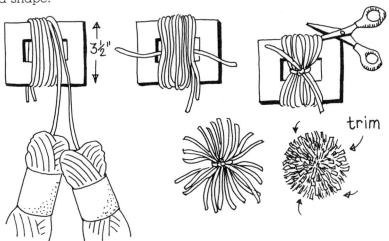

Fabric sacks and drawstring bags

If you have a sewing machine, fabric sacks and drawstring bags are excellent solutions to gift wrap problems of all shapes and sizes. You can make a sack or bag tiny enough for a pearl or big enough for a banjo, a grandfather clock or a pair of skis. The basic bag is quick and easy to stitch up from fabric remnants plus ribbon or cord. You might make a calico sack with pinked calico ribbon, satin drawstring bag with silver cord, muslin sack with gingham ribbon, pinwale corduroy drawstring bag with plaid taffeta ribbon, even a bandanna sack with contrasting bandanna ribbon.

Fabric sacks

A sack is made of two pieces of fabric stitched together on three sides. To determine the size of each piece, first measure loosely around the widest part of the gift. Add 4 inches to the measurement and then divide by two. This is the width. For the height, measure the gift from center bottom to center top and add 6 inches. With pinking shears, cut two pieces of fabric to these measurements. Hold the pieces with right sides together and stitch down one side, across the bottom and up the other side with ½-inch seam allowances, as shown in the drawing. Turn right side out and iron.

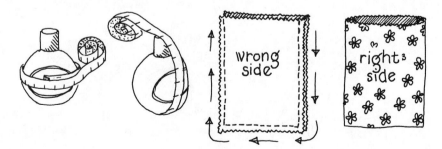

Wrap the gift in tissue paper if you like and slip it into the sack. Gather the top together as if it were tied. If there is too much extra fabric at the top, trim carefully with pinking shears. If you are using velvet, satin or some other fabric that ravels easily, turn under and stitch a narrow hem at the top.

When the top edge is completed, gather the fabric together, tie tightly with ribbon and make a bow. If you are using narrow ribbon, cord or yarn, wind it around the fabric several times before tying and making the bow.

Drawstring bags

A drawstring bag is made of two pieces of fabric stitched together on one side, the bottom and part of the other side. To determine the size of each piece, first measure loosely around the widest part of the gift. Add 4 inches to the measurement and then divide by two. This is the width. For the height, measure the gift from center bottom to center top and add 4 inches. Cut two pieces of fabric to these measurements.

With right sides together, stitch down one side, across the bottom and up the other side, ending the stitching 2½ inches from the top edge of the fabric as shown in the drawing. Press open the side seams. Turn down the top edge 1½ inches and press the fold. Turn the bag right side out and press. To make the casing for the ribbon, stitch around the top 1 inch from the folded edge through both layers of fabric. This casing will accommodate any ribbon or cord up to 1-inch wide.

Thread ribbon or cord through the casing: Pin a large safety pin to one end of the ribbon and inch it through the casing, pulling the ribbon along behind. Allow plenty of ribbon for a generous bow. Wrap the gift in tissue paper if you like and slip it into the bag. Gather the top of the bag on the ribbon, tie and make a bow.

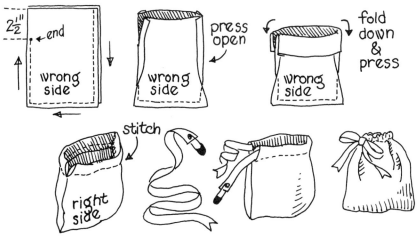

Do-it-yourself gift cards and tags

A gift card is usually larger than a tag, with more room for your message, and has an envelope. A tag has no envelope and may have room for writing only the recipient's name and your name. Any card or tag may be slipped into the gift box or other gift container before wrapping, but if you wish to attach it to the outside of the package (making it an element of the design), check page 42 for the best methods. You should also browse through Chapter 5 to see a variety of gift tags used on a variety of packages.

Use any of the following unlined, blank papers as the foundations for making cards: ready-made plain folded notes with matching envelopes from the stationery store or five-and-ten; index cards folded in half, tucked into envelopes; solid-color stationery, folded in half, with matching envelopes; construction paper or other artist's paper folded and cut to fit in any envelope you have on hand.

Use any of the following unlined, blank pieces of paper as the foundations for making tags: ready-made tags from the stationery store (see page 13); 3″ × 5″ or 4″ × 6″ index cards cut down or folded in half; small pieces of 2-ply Bristol board or any other heavy artist's paper cut down to the size of your choice. If the tag has no loop, you will need to add one: punch a hole at the top or the upper left corner and thread a short length of thin string, yarn or cord through the hole; tie the ends in a knot.

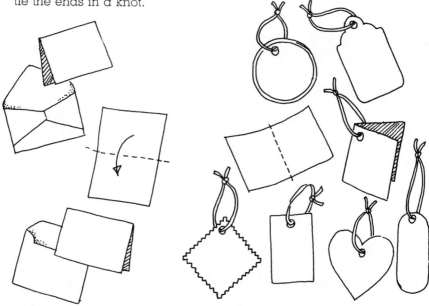

Cut-paper designs

You will need: cards and/or tags as described on page 52; package of origami paper; either spray adhesive or white glue and a small artist's brush

Fold a sheet of origami paper in half, quarters or sixths, with the wrong side of the paper out. Draw a design in pencil, making sure the finished, unfolded paper cut will fit on your card or tag. Carefully cut out the design and unfold. Using spray adhesive or white glue applied with the small brush, glue the design to the front of the card or tag. The drawings below will give you some ideas.

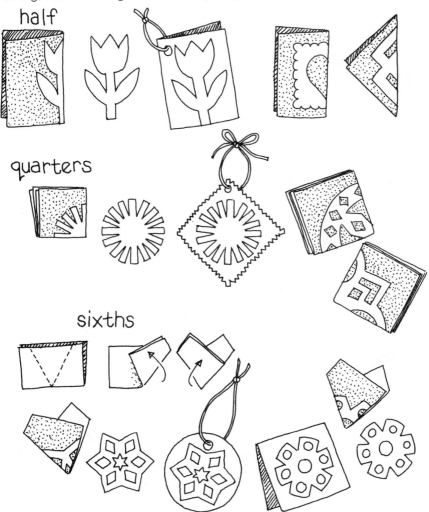

Mosaic designs

You will need: cards and/or tags as described on page 52; assorted colors of construction paper; white glue and a small artist's brush

Cut the construction paper into ½-inch squares; if you cut up half a small sheet each of four or five colors, you will have enough squares for several cards or tags. Glue the squares to the cards and tags in geometric designs as shown below: first arrange the squares on the card; then lift each square, apply glue to the back and replace it in position on the card.

Folded designs

You will need: construction paper or any other firm, colored paper; felt-tip markers; sequins, bits of ribbon and lace, odds and ends of rickrack and other decorative trims; white glue

Fish, fan, heart, pumpkin, Christmas wreath, wedge of birthday cake—draw any of these on a folded sheet of construction paper, incorporating the fold into the design as shown below. Cut out, decorate and write your message inside. Slip into an envelope if you wish or just tuck under the gift wrap ribbon.

Applied designs

This is a catch-all term that means anything glued to the front of your cards and tags. The list of possible appliqués is long; here is a selection.

● Flowers, vegetables or fruits cut from seed packets or seed catalogues

● Parts of doilies (try white on dark paper, gold or silver on bright-colored paper)

● Stickers or seals arranged in geometric designs

● Heart, star or dove from Chapter 4 (make them from pretty gift wrap or other patterned paper)

● Motifs cut from the front or inside of used greeting cards

● Delicious-looking dishes cut from gourmet magazines or catalogues

● Motifs cut from fabric

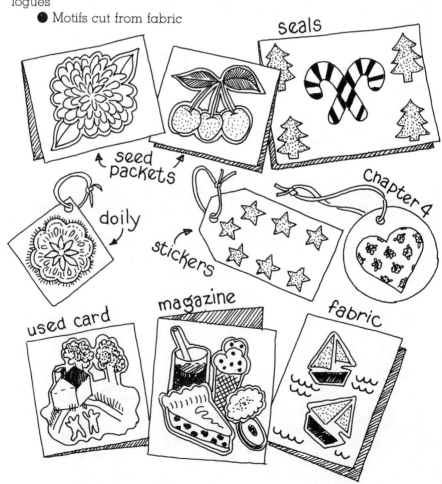

CHAPTER 4
Portfolio of Patterns

On the following pages you will find a selection of fourteen patterns that can be used in dozens of ways in your gift wrap designs. Throughout the book there are references to these patterns and ideas for using them; there is also a list of suggestions on page 58. The instructions below show you how to transfer each pattern to cardboard to make a template; the template can then be outlined on paper, fabric or even cookie dough.

How to transfer a pattern to make a template

1. Place a piece of tracing paper over a pattern in the book. With a pencil or pen, copy the pattern onto the tracing paper.

2. Put a sheet of ordinary carbon paper, ink side down, on a piece of heavy paper or thin cardboard. (Use a file folder, index card, piece of poster board, oaktag, etc.) Place the tracing paper on top of the carbon paper and draw firmly over the outline with pencil or ball-point pen.

3. Remove the tracing and carbon papers and cut out the transferred pattern on the black outline. This cut-out is the template.

How to use templates in gift wrap designs

● Gift tag: Outline any template on card-weight paper. Cut out and decorate with gummed stickers or felt-tip markers, leaving room in the middle for writing the recipient's name. Punch a hole at the top and tie to the bow on the gift.

● Gift tag: Fold a piece of construction paper in half. Place the teddy bear template on the paper, with the hand and foot overlapping the fold slightly. Outline the template and cut on the outline through both layers. Write the name of the recipient on the front and a message inside. Glue the back of the tag to the wrapped gift.

● Package trim: Accordion-fold a piece of thin paper. Outline the tree, gingerbread boy or girl, snowflake or heart on the top fold, making sure that the template overlaps both side edges of the paper. Cut out through all layers and unfold. Glue the chain to the package. (See wrap #7, page 72, for an example of this usage.)

● Package trim: Outline the flower template on a pretty color of felt and cut out. Glue sequins in the center. Outline the leaf template twice on green felt and cut out with pinking shears. Glue the leaves so they peek out from behind the flower and glue the flower (or several flowers) to the wrapped package.

● Package trim: Outline the small and large heart templates on red paper and the medium heart on pink or gold paper. Glue together in a stack. Glue the stack to a paper doily and glue the doily to a Valentine's Day gift wrapping.

● Package appliqué: Outline the dove template twice on calico fabric, once facing each direction. Outline the wing twice on matching solid-color fabric and glue to the doves. Glue the doves to a yarn-tied package.

Small, medium and large hearts

Flower

Dove

Snowflake

Gingerbread boy and girl

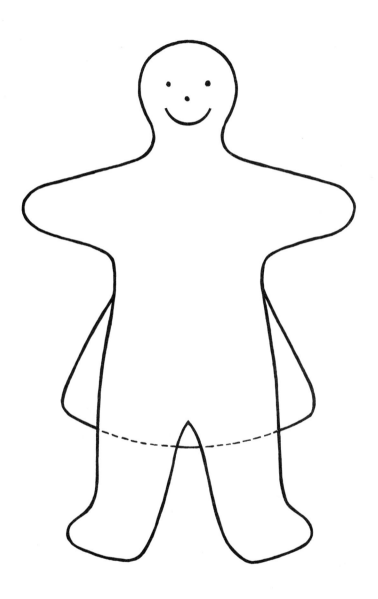

Teddy bear

Holly leaf

Christmas tree

Small and large stars

Leaf

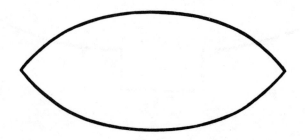

CHAPTER 5
Fifty Great Wraps
and How to Do Them

In this chapter you will find complete instructions for fifty different designs—gift wraps for a variety of occasions and holidays, gift wraps for boxes, bags, envelopes and tins. Use these designs as suggested in the text and drawings or adapt them to your particular needs. For example, one of the Valentine's Day wraps might be just right for Aunt Joan's birthday, while the gardener's wrap (#17) might suit your mom perfectly on Mother's Day.

Do take liberties with these designs: convert a wrapping design for a large box into a design for a small box; take an idea from a box and adapt it for a shopping bag. Feel free to make appropriate substitutions in materials, too: yarn instead of cord; patterned paper instead of solid-color paper; apparel ribbon instead of gift wrap ribbon. Keep in mind the possibilities offered in Chapter 3 (*Do It Yourself: Making Your Own Materials*). There are papers, ribbons, fabric sacks, envelopes, gift tags and cards you may want to incorporate into these gift wraps. With a little imagination and flexibility you can multiply fifty great wraps into fifty more great wraps.

#1: Birthday

Special delivery

You will need: white paper with matte finish; small snapshot of the recipient; 2 felt-tip markers; FIRST CLASS postal stickers

Wrap the box neatly with white paper. Cut the border of the snapshot in small scallops to make it look as if the edges were perforated. Glue the snapshot to the upper right corner of the box. Using one color of felt-tip marker, write the givers' names and address in the upper left corner. Using the second felt-tip marker, write the recipient's name and address in the middle of the box. Decorate with FIRST CLASS stickers.

#2: Birthday

Dots with dash

You will need: shiny paper sack; self-adhesive dots, ⅜ inch in diameter; 2 pieces of cord for the handle; gift tag with string loop

Apply dots to the front of the sack, spelling out the recipient's name and decorating the upper and lower edges. Wrap your gift in tissue paper and put it in the sack. Fold down the corners of the sack as shown in the drawing and punch holes through all layers. Thread the ends of the two pieces of cord through one hole and tie a knot. Slip the gift tag onto the cords and thread the ends of the cord through the other hole. Adjust the length to make the handle, tie another knot and clip off excess cord.

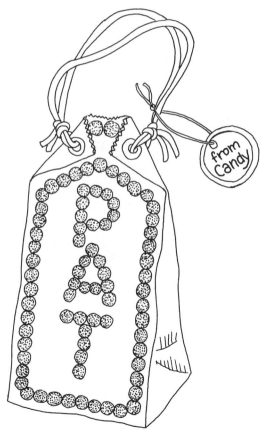

#3: Birthday

Ribbon bouquet

You will need: gift wrap; several colors of matching or contrasting satin sheen gift wrap ribbon, ¾ to 1 inch wide, including green; 9 to 12 small or medium pompons cut from ball fringe

Wrap the box neatly in gift wrap and satin sheen ribbon, taping the ribbon on the back of the box. Following the instructions on page 38, make three Flower Bows. Tape or glue the bows to the package as shown.

#4: Birthday

Rickrack trimming

You will need: shiny, solid-color gift wrap; gold or silver self-ad-hesive (sometimes called *stick-to*) craft trim; medium rickrack; gift tag trimmed with rickrack and a pompon cut from ball fringe, with a string loop; yarn pompon (page 49)

Wrap the box neatly with shiny paper. Apply craft trim to the top of the box, at right angles, running it down the sides and ending on the back of the box. Glue or tape rickrack parallel to the craft trim, ending neatly on the back of the box. Tape the loop of the gift tag to the top of the box at the intersection of the trims. Glue the pompon over the intersection, concealing the piece of tape.

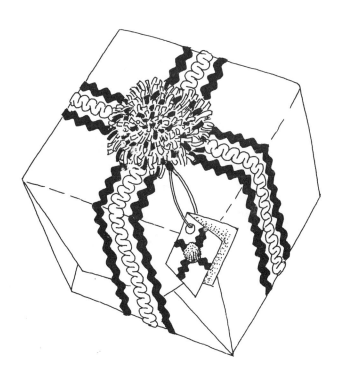

#5: Child's birthday

A winning bear

You will need: paper shopping bag; construction paper or felt for the bear; small piece of ribbon for the bow tie; medium pompons (cut from ball fringe) for the paws; small buttons for the eyes and nose; bit of yarn for the mouth; jumbo rickrack for the border; gift tag with string loop

Using the pattern in Chapter 4 (page 62), cut a teddy bear out of construction paper or felt. Glue the bear to the center of one side of the shopping bag. Decorate the bear with the trims listed above, as shown in the drawing. Glue pieces of jumbo rickrack around the bear. Wrap the gift in tissue paper and place it in the shopping bag. Tie the gift tag to the handle.

#6: Child's birthday

Sticker tapes

You will need: solid-color gift wrap; strips of self-adhesive stickers; gift card

Wrap the box neatly with gift wrap. Cross two strips of stickers over the top of the box, wrap them around and tape securely on the back. Make two loops of stickers, cross them at right angles and staple them to the strips on top of the box. Cover the staple with a sticker. Write your message on the gift card and attach it to the box with another sticker.

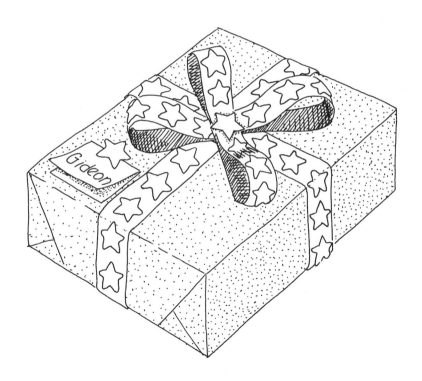

#7: Child's birthday

Paper chains

**You will need: gift wrap in a small prin., t or solid color; brown
construction paper; matching or contrasting ribbon**

Wrap the box neatly in paper. Make a chain of gingerbread folks:
Accordion-fold a piece of construction paper. On the top fold draw a
gingerbread boy or girl freehand (or use the pattern on page 61). Cut
out through all layers, leaving the linked hands intact. Unfold the
chain and position it across the top of the box as shown. Make as
many gingerbread folks as needed to reach all the way across. Draw
the eyes, noses, mouths and buttons with felt-tip markers. Glue the
chains in place. If the box has deep sides, make more chains and glue
around the sides, too. Make a gift tag from one fold of a chain: decorate
the front; write your message inside; punch a hole and loop a piece
of string through the hole. Wrap the ribbon around the box just above
the gingerbread folks and tie a knot. Slip the gift tag loop onto the
ribbon and then tie the ribbon in a bow.

#8: Child's birthday

Rainbow balloons

You will need: gift wrap in a bright print; contrasting chubby yarn; 8 to 10 balloons; twist tie or small piece of thin wire

Wrap the box neatly in the bright paper. Tie up with chubby yarn, make two knots and then make a bow. Holding the bow up out of the way, group the ends of the balloons under the bow, spaced evenly around it as shown in the drawing. Secure the ends with a twist tie or piece of wire.

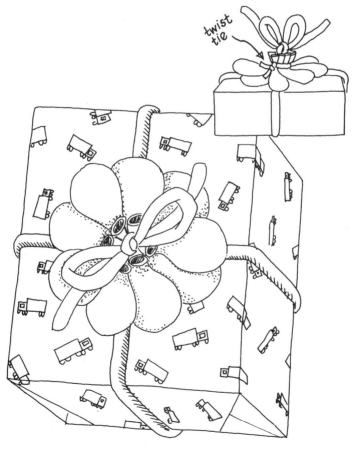

#9: Baby shower

Dainty ruffles and ribbons

You will need: mushroom basket from the greengrocer or other basket from the five-and-ten; white spray paint or white acrylic paint; white beading (gathered eyelet with slots along the heading for threading a ribbon); satin ribbon in a pretty pastel for the beading, the bow and the lower edge

Clean the basket if necessary and apply two coats of white paint, letting each coat dry thoroughly. Measure around the top edge of the basket and cut a piece of beading and a piece of ribbon to that measurement. Thread the ribbon through the beading and glue around the top edge of the basket beginning and ending at the center back. Glue ribbon around the lower edge of the basket, beginning and ending at center back. Make a Medallion Bow (page 34) and glue it in place at center front. Fill the basket with small wrapped gifts nestled in a bed of white tissue paper.

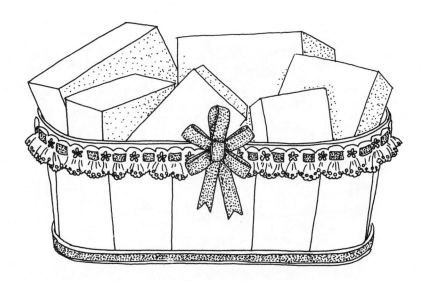

#10: New baby

Take a baby step

You will need: gift wrap in a baby-shower pattern; narrow satin ribbon in 2 or 3 matching or contrasting colors; heavy-weight colored paper for the bootees; small piece of gathered lace and 2 small pompons cut from ball fringe

Wrap the box neatly in paper. Enlarge the gridded baby bootee diagram below, cut out the pattern and outline it twice on the colored paper. Cut out the two bootees and punch a hole in the corner of each. Glue lace and a pompon to each bootee. Thread a short loop of narrow ribbon through the holes and tie the ends in a knot. Tie up the box with the two or three satin ribbons, working with them as if they were one strand, and make a knot (no bow yet). Slip the loop of the bootees onto the ribbons and then tie a bow. Write your message on one of the bootees.

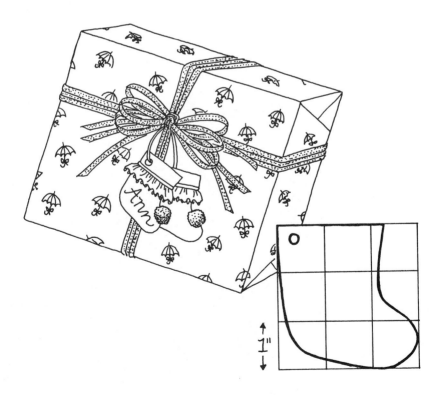

#11: Bon voyage

Don't forget to write

You will need: kraft paper; navy blue, dark red or dark brown gros-grain apparel ribbon, 1 inch wide, for the straps; matching ribbon, ¼ inch wide, for the bows; 2 chenille pipe cleaners; luggage tag or gift tag with string loop; postal stickers

Wrap the package neatly in kraft paper. Stand it on its side like a suitcase; the side is now the bottom. To make the straps, wrap two ribbons around the box, parallel and about 5 inches apart, and tape securely on the bottom. Twist the pipe cleaners together and shape into a handle as shown. Tuck each end of the handle under a ribbon at the top of the box with dabs of glue to hold the handle in place and upright. When the glue is dry, tie a ribbon bow to each side of the handle, slipping the luggage or gift tag onto one of the ribbons. Decorate the suitcase with postal stickers.

#12: Housewarming

Welcome home

You will need: gift wrap that resembles wallpaper (geometric pattern, narrow stripe, tiny flowers); small piece of fabric or felt for the rug; narrow fringe for the rug trim; unlined 3″ × 5″ index card; bits of ribbon for the frame; yarn or cord in a contrasting color; miniature chair (e.g., from a dollhouse)

Wrap the box neatly with paper. Cut the fabric or felt into an oval that will fit on the lower part of the box. Glue fringe around the edge of the oval. Glue the rug to the box. Fold the index card in half and glue the back to the upper right corner of the box. Glue mitered pieces of ribbon around the card to make a frame. Write "Home Sweet Home" on the top of the card and your name and message inside. Tie the cord around the box and make a knot, slightly off center as shown in the drawing. Slip the miniature chair onto the cord and tie a bow.

#13: Engagement or wedding shower
Wishing you every joy

You will need: gift wrap in a solid color or a quiet pattern; 2 matching or contrasting colors of satin sheen gift wrap ribbon that sticks to itself when moistened (Color A and Color B); 2 pipe cleaners; a variety of artificial flowers; small gift tag with string loop

Wrap the box neatly with gift wrap. To make a medium-size woven basket, cut four pieces of Color A, each 6 inches long. Cut seven pieces of Color B, each 3½ inches long. Weave the ribbons together, moistening at the intersections, to make a rectangle. Trim off the excess ribbon at the edges and trim the sides at a slight angle. Twist the pipe cleaners together as shown and shape them to make the basket handle. Glue the basket and handle to the package. Cut flowers from their stems and glue above the basket; glue two or three small flowers over the joint of the pipe cleaners. Glue the string of the gift tag to the handle.

#14: Wedding, engagement or anniversary

Honor the happy couple

You will need: gift wrap in a small print, dot, stripe or solid color; contrasting wide ribbon; construction paper; bits of ribbon, felt, tiny buttons, pearls, rickrack, etc.; bright-color glitter pen

Wrap the package neatly with gift wrap. Tie the ribbon on the diagonal, ending with a big bow (see page 29). Using the girl and boy patterns in Chapter 4 (page 61), cut figures out of construction paper. Glue the figures to the top of the box. Dress and decorate the couple with trims: felt shirt, ribbon tie, button shoes, pearl necklace, rickrack belt, etc. Draw the faces with felt-tip pens and don't forget yarn hair. Write the names with glitter pen.

#15: Anniversary

For our favorite lovebirds

You will need: gift wrap (try do-it-yourself paper, pages 44–46); 2 colors of construction paper or other heavy colored paper; contrasting ribbon for the bow

Wrap the box neatly with gift wrap. Using the dove pattern from Chapter 4 (page 60), cut out two doves from one color of construction paper. Draw the wings and eyes with felt-tip pen. Place the doves in position on the package. Using the small or medium heart pattern (page 59) and the second color of paper, cut out and arrange as many hearts as you need to make an arch over the doves. Write your message in tiny printing on one of the hearts. Make a Flat Loops Bow (page 36) and position it under the doves. When all the elements are arranged to your satisfaction, glue the bow in place and attach the doves and hearts with tape loops.

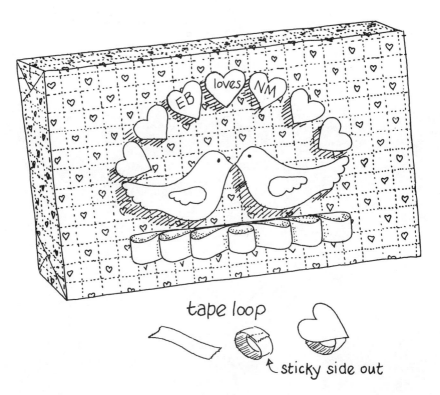

tape loop

sticky side out

#16: Silver or golden wedding anniversary

Warm memories and best wishes

You will need: gift wrap in silver or gold, perhaps with an embossed pattern; double-face white satin ribbon about 1¼ to 1½ inches wide; several stems of artificial lilies of the valley

Wrap the box neatly with paper. Arrange the ribbon at right angles as shown and tape or glue on the front and back of the box. Glue the stems of the lilies of the valley at the intersection of the ribbon. Make a Medallion Bow (page 34) and glue it in place over the stems.

#17: Gift for a gardener

The greenest thumb in town

**You will need: gift wrap in a small print, dot, stripe or solid color;
2 stretch ties; green felt-tip marker; white gardening glove; construction paper; green pipe cleaner; double-face tape; 4 packets of seeds
(if the box is large enough to accommodate them as shown)**

Wrap the box neatly in paper. Stretch the ties over the opposite
corners. Using the green marker, color the tip of the thumb of the
gardening glove. Cut a flower out of construction paper (draw freehand or use the pattern on page 59) and tape the end of the pipe
cleaner to the back of the flower. Position the glove on the box and
attach it with double-face tape. Tape the pipe cleaner stem to the
glove. Bring the index finger and thumb over the pipe cleaner and
secure with double-face tape. Write your message over the petals of
the flower. Tuck the seed packets under the stretch ties. Don't forget
to present the gardener with the other glove!

#18: Gift for a needleworker

The craftiest hand around

You will need: solid-color shopping bag in shiny or matte finish; jumbo rickrack; medium ball fringe; gift tag with paper mosaic design (page 54), with string loop

Glue two pieces of rickrack to the front of the bag, several inches apart. Glue ball fringe around the top edge of the bag. Cut pompons from the remaining ball fringe and glue them randomly in the space between the pieces of rickrack. Wrap your gift in tissue paper and tuck it into the shopping bag. Tie the gift tag to the handle.

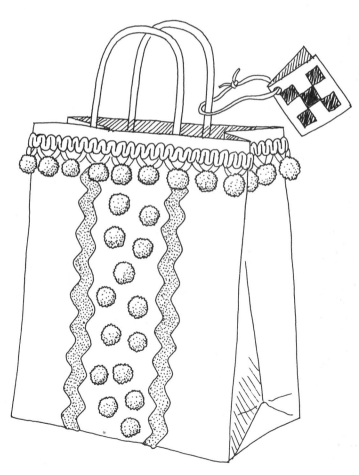

#19: Gift for a cook

My favorite chef

You will need: gift wrap in a stripe, dot or solid color; magazines with pictures of delicious food (try one of the gourmet magazines); curling ribbon; measuring spoons on a ring; blank gift tag with string loop

Wrap the box neatly with paper. Cut out pictures of food and glue them randomly over the top and sides of the box. Glue one picture to the front of the blank gift tag. Using several strands of curling ribbon as if they were one, tie up the box, making a knot on top. Slip the ring of the measuring spoons and the loop of the gift tag onto one of the ribbons and then tie the ribbons in a bow. Curl the ends of the ribbon over the blade of a scissors.

#20: Gift for a sailor

A great old salt

You will need: shiny blue gift wrap; one silver stretch tie; origami paper or construction paper

Wrap the box neatly with blue paper. Put the stretch tie around the box. Make several paper pennants with geometric designs as shown in the drawing. Fold the end of each pennant around the stretch tie and glue in place. Write your message on one of the pennants.

#21: All occasions

Extra! Wrapping makes headlines

You will need: newspapers; paper ribbons (page 47) made from bright colors of shiny gift wrap

Newspapers make fine gift wrap, especially when you're pinched for time or cash. You can match the paper to the recipient (stock market pages for the business person, comics for the kids) or match it to the gift (recipe pages to wrap kitchen equipment, science news around a microscope). For a big gift, simply glue several sheets of newspaper together to make one very large piece of wrapping paper.

Wrap the box neatly. Tape paper ribbons around the package and top with paper curls or a Simple Loops Bow (page 31), made from paper ribbons.

#22: All occasions

The more, the merrier

You will need: 2 different but coordinated gift wraps, perhaps one patterned and one solid color or a geometric pattern and a stripe in coordinated colors; wide florist's ribbon or wide apparel ribbon

This is a wrapping for a gift made up of several boxes—it might be several items for a new baby or a collection of exotic foods for your neighbors at Christmas. Before wrapping any of the boxes, stack them in a pyramid. Take alternate boxes and wrap them in one gift wrap; wrap the remaining boxes in the second gift wrap. Restack the wrapped boxes with two tape loops between each pair, to hold them in place and keep them from sliding around. Carefully tie up the entire stack with ribbon, ending with a knot on top. Clip off the excess ribbon in points as shown. Make a big Crisp Full Bow (page 32) or a Fluffy Bow (page 33) and glue or tape it to the top of the stack of gifts.

#23: All occasions

Display a favorite painting

You will need: manila envelope; small art print or postcard; several strands of cord in colors that match the print; gift tag with string loop

This wrapping is for a relatively flat gift that fits comfortably in an envelope. Glue the print or postcard to the front of the envelope, centering it neatly. Wrap the gift in tissue paper if necessary and slip it all the way into the envelope. Fold down the flap and punch two holes near the top edge. Thread the cord through the holes, slip the loop of the gift tag onto one end of the cord and tie a bow.

#24: All occasions

Make it stylish and elegant

You will need: solid-color gift wrap; patterned gift wrap; contrasting satin sheen gift wrap ribbon; 3 or 4 small pompons cut from ball fringe; gift tag

This is a wrapping for a cylindrical gift. Wrap the cylinder neatly in solid-color gift wrap, following the instructions on page 24. Cover the ends of the package with glued-on circles of patterned gift wrap. Cut a square of patterned gift wrap that will fit on the front of the cylinder as shown in the drawing. Glue it, centered, to the front of the cylinder. Make a Flower Bow (page 38), omitting the leaves. Use white glue to adhere the bow to another piece of ribbon; let the glue dry. Attach the bow by wrapping the ribbon around the cylinder, knotting or taping the ends on the back. Clip off any excess ribbon. Tuck the gift tag between the ribbon and the patterned gift wrap.

#25: All occasions

Curl a cluster of ribbons

You will need: gift wrap; several matching or contrasting colors of curling ribbon; yarn pompon (page 49)

This is a wrapping for a tall, square box. Wrap the box neatly in paper, following the instructions on page 23. Cut 10 to 15 pieces of curling ribbon of varying lengths. Glue the ribbons one by one to the top of the box as shown in the diagram. When the glue is dry, carefully curl each end of ribbon by drawing it along the blade of a scissors. Glue the pompon over the center of the ribbons.

glue

#26: All occasions

Wrap it in fabric

You will need: either a square of pretty fabric with the edges pinked or a napkin, scarf, bandanna or tea towel; 2 twist ties; gold, silver or other color cord; dried flowers; gift tag with string loop

This wrapping is for any cylindrical gift. The size of the fabric you will need depends on the size of the cylinder. Lay the fabric (napkin, scarf, etc.) flat and roll up the cylinder in it. Twist each end snugly over the gift and secure with a twist tie. Wrap one end of the cord two or three times around one twist tie to cover it and make a knot. Stretch the long end of the cord down over the cylinder and wrap it two or three times around the second twist tie, catching the stems of a small group of dried flowers and the loop of a gift tag as you wrap. Work the end of the cord around to knot it. Cut off excess cord.

#27: All Occasions

Keep it simple and pretty

You will need: 2 colors of tissue paper; cord; gift tag with string loop; small bunch of dried flowers

This is a wrapping for a jar. Using one color of tissue paper, cut a square large enough to cover the top of the jar as shown in the drawing. Using the second color, cut a square about ½ inch smaller. Center the smaller square on the larger and place them over the top of the jar. Slip the gift tag onto the cord and wrap the cord two or three times around the jar just below the lid, gathering the tissue paper neatly; knot once. Tie the cord over the small bunch of dried flowers and knot again. Cut off the excess cord.

#28: All occasions

Add something extra

You will need: gift wrap; ribbon; extra little present

This is the add-a-gift wrap, a way to make any gift extra special by attaching an extra little present. Simply wrap the main gift and tie it up with ribbon, making a knot but no bow. Tie the ends of ribbon around or through the extra little present and then make a bow.

Here are some suggestions for the extra present:

package of appliqués
skeins of crewel yarn
sewing kit
miniature tool kit
small flashlight
tiny books
packet of bookplates
packet of notecards
box of crayons
colored pencils or markers
sealing wax
address book
package of origami paper
small paintbox
wooden spoons
pretty potholder
seed packets
new calendar
special key ring

miniature car or airplane
bicycle bell or horn
harmonica
noisemaker
mask or funny face
theatrical makeup
tarot cards
puzzles
bag of marbles
small stuffed animal
small doll
card of barrettes
pretty stickpin
sachet
special soap
jazzy shoelaces
roll of film
tape cartridge
argyle socks

#29: All occasions

Quick and easy stitching

You will need: kraft paper; hole puncher; 2 colors of 4-ply yarn; yarn needle

This wrapping is for a record. With pinking shears, cut two pieces of brown paper, each 14 inches square. Holding the two pieces together, mark with pencil and then punch ten holes on each side, about ½ inch from the pinked edge (see drawing). Cut four pieces of each color of yarn, each piece 42 inches long. Hold two pieces of yarn together (one of each color) and thread through the yarn needle. Stitch through the holes on two sides as shown, adjusting the yarn ends so you have equal lengths of excess yarn at the beginning and end. Slip the record between the two squares of paper. Stitch up the remaining sides as described above. Tie the ends of yarn in bows in the center of each side. Glue pieces of yarn spelling out the recipient's name.

#30: All occasions

American country look

You will need: solid-color, dotted or small-print gift wrap; gingham or grosgrain apparel ribbon or calico craft ribbon; construction paper; a few stalks of wheat and a few dried flowers; small length of yarn; gift tag with string loop

Wrap the box neatly with gift wrap. Position the ribbon as shown in the drawing and tape on the back of the box. Using the pattern in Chapter 4 (page 60), cut two doves out of construction paper. Draw the wings and eyes with felt-tip marker. Make an arrangement of wheat stalks and dried flowers as shown, cutting the stems down to size. Tie in the center with yarn, slip the tag onto the yarn and make a bow. Glue the arrangement to the box and glue the doves above the arrangement.

#31: Valentine's Day

A heart full of love

**You will need: gift wrap in a Valentine's Day or flowered pattern;
matching double-face satin ribbon about 1 inch wide for the box and
the bow; small bunch of artificial flowers; gathered trim, e.g., crystal
pleating, box-pleated lace, gathered eyelet**

Wrap the box neatly in paper and ribbon, gluing or taping the
ribbon on the back of the box. Make a Medallion Bow (page 34), leaving off the center loop of ribbon, and glue it over the ribbons. Glue
the bunch of flowers over the bow. Glue gathered trim in the shape
of a heart around the bow and flowers as shown below. Snip off excess
trim at the bottom point of the heart.

#32: Valentine's Day

Sweetheart, be mine

You will need: gift wrap in a romantic pattern; square or rectangular white doily (depending on the shape of the box); picot-edge apparel ribbon about 1 inch wide, for the box and the bow; heart stickers

Wrap the box neatly with paper. Wrap ribbon around the length and width of the box and tape it on the back. Cut the solid paper center out of the doily and glue the remaining frame of lace to the top of the box. Make a Flat Loops Bow (page 36) and glue it over the ribbon on the center top of the box. Add heart stickers around the bow or on the doily.

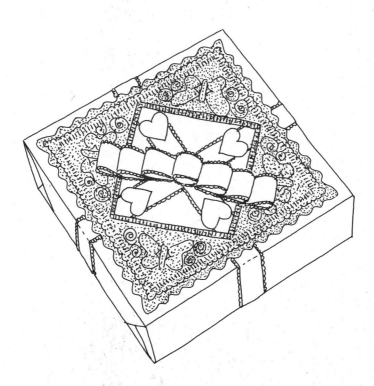

#33: Easter

Scrambled eggs

You will need: shiny paper sack; assorted colors of origami paper or other colored paper; 3 pieces (3 colors) of yarn or cord

Using different colors of paper, cut out an assortment of small eggs and glue them to the front of the paper sack as shown in the drawing. Cut three paper circles of graduated sizes; the diameter of the largest circle should be the width of the paper sack plus ½ inch. Stack the circles, centered, and fold the stack in half. Put a tissue-wrapped gift in the sack and fold the top down neatly about 2 inches. Place the stack of paper circles over the folded top of the sack. Punch two holes through all the layers. Thread the yarn through the holes and tie a bow.

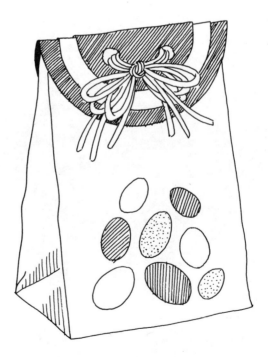

#34: Easter

Easter basket

You will need: Easter basket with handle; unlined 5″ × 8″ index card for the bunny; small gift, wrapped neatly in paper; green cellophane grass; wide florist's ribbon for the bow; gift tag with string loop; foil-covered chocolate eggs or other Easter candy

Fold the index card in half the long way. Draw the bunny on the folded card, following the diagram on the grid below. Cut out through both layers of card and fold the legs forward as indicated by the heavy lines. Draw a face on the bunny. Put the gift in the basket and cover with grass. Knot the ribbon on the handle of the basket, slip the loop of the tag onto one end of ribbon and then tie a bow. Stand the bunny on the grass and tape the paw to the handle so the bunny stands upright. Pile eggs or candies on the grass.

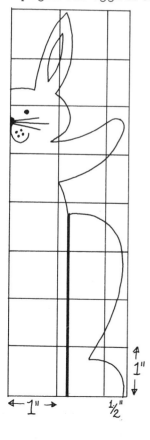

1″

1″   ½″

#35: Mother's Day

For my favorite mom

You will need: gift wrap in a small print, dot or geometric pattern; contrasting narrow velvet ribbon; enough artificial flowers to make a small nosegay; gift tag with string loop

Wrap the box neatly with paper. Cut two equal lengths of ribbon, each long enough to wrap around the box and tie in a bow. Keeping them parallel, with right sides out, wrap each ribbon around the box and tie a knot on the center top. Group the stems of the flowers over the knots and tie one ribbon in a bow over the stems, securing them. Slip the loop of the gift tag onto the second ribbon and tie the second ribbon in a bow over the stems, too. Try to keep the right sides of the ribbon facing out when you make the bows. Clip off the excess ribbon.

#36: Father's Day

For my good old dad

You will need: instant camera; gift wrap; wide ribbon in a color contrasting with the gift wrap; 2 pieces of cord or yarn

First make a big sign: write "Happy Father's Day" with paint or wide felt-tip marker on a big piece of paper. Gather the family around the sign and have a friend or neighbor take an instant photograph. Wrap the gift box neatly with paper. Glue the photograph to the box and glue ribbon around the photograph to make a frame. Tie the ends of the two pieces of cord together to make a bow. Glue the bow above the frame and glue the dangling cords to the box, ending at the corners of the frame. Cut off any excess cord.

#37: Graduation

On your red-letter day

You will need: gift wrap; unused calendar page with the day, month and year of the important date; gift wrap ribbons

Wrap the box neatly with paper. Center the calendar page on top of the box and draw around it with pencil. Line up four lengths of ribbon centered on the pencil lines as shown and glue them to the box or tape them securely on the back of the box. Glue the calendar page over the ribbon. Make a Twisted Loops Bow (page 37) and glue it at the top of the calendar page. Circle the important date in red.

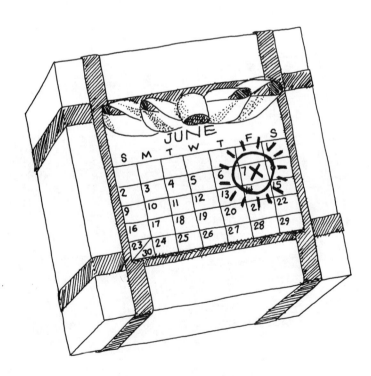

#38: Halloween

Boo!

You will need: brown paper bag about 8 inches high and 5 to 6 inches wide; 48 inches of orange craft, florist's or apparel ribbon; orange and green construction paper

Halloween treats and goodies will go in this decorated bag. To make the handles, cut two pieces of ribbon, each 12 inches long. Use white glue to attach the ends of one piece to the inside of one side of the bag, each end extending 2 inches down into the bag. Repeat with the second piece of ribbon on the other side of the bag. Cut the remaining ribbon in four equal pieces and tie a knot in the center of each piece. Glue the knotted pieces at the top edge of the bag as shown in the drawing. Cut a pumpkin out of orange construction paper. Cut out eyes, nose and mouth. Cut a green stem and glue it behind the center top of the pumpkin. Glue the pumpkin to the center front of the bag.

#39 Chanukah

For the Festival of Lights

You will need: shiny blue gift wrap; 2 gold stretch ties; white satin or grosgrain ribbon about ¼ to ⅜ inch wide; metallic gold ribbon about 1 inch wide

Wrap the box neatly with blue paper. Stretch the gold ties over opposite corners. For the candles, cut eight pieces of white ribbon all the same length and one piece about an inch longer. Arrange them on the top of the box as shown in the drawing. For the menorah, cut one piece of gold ribbon for the horizontal arm and a second piece for the vertical. Cut nine gold ribbon diamonds to represent the flames. Glue all the pieces to the box.

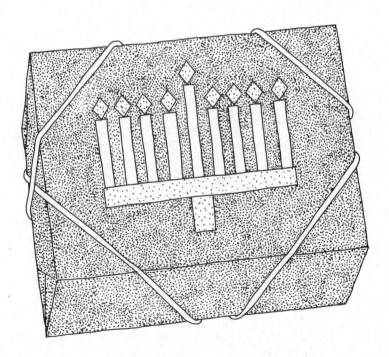

#40: Chanukah

Come spin the dreidel

You will need: gift wrap; 4 pieces of construction paper; 2 pieces of thin cord; wooden bead with large hole; gift card

Wrap the box neatly with gift wrap. Using the pattern as a guide, cut out four dreidels and glue one at each corner of the top of the package. Center and cross the cords on the bottom of the box and tape them to the box at the intersection. Bring the ends of the cord up around the four sides to the top of the box. Slip the ends through the hole of the wooden bead and push the bead down. Divide the four cords into pairs, knot and tie a bow. Clip off the excess cord. Tuck the gift card under the bead.

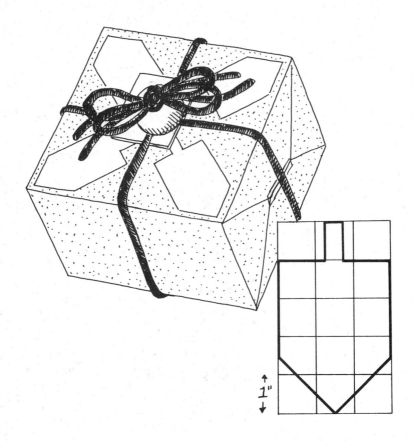

#41: Christmas

Jolly green trees

You will need: holiday gift wrap (any do-it-yourself paper, pages 44–46, would be a good choice for this wrapping); green paper for the trees (shiny gift wrap or construction paper); 4 large pompons cut from ball fringe, in a contrasting color; satin sheen gift wrap ribbon in a contrasting color for the bow; gift tag with string loop

This wrapping is for a tall box. Wrap the box neatly with paper. Using the tree pattern from Chapter 4, page 63, cut out four green trees. Glue each tree to one side of the box. Top each tree with a glued-on pompon. Make Variation #2 or #3 of the Simple Loops Bow (page 31) or make the Fluffy Bow (page 33) and glue it to the top of the box. Tape the strings of the tag out of sight under the bow.

#42: Christmas

Silvery glitter and sparkle

You will need: gift wrap in a deep, solid color like royal blue or pine green; silver satin sheen ribbon; silver glitter pen

Wrap the box neatly with the solid-color paper. Tie up the box with silver ribbon, ending with a knot. Make a Fluffy Bow (page 33) and tape or glue it in position. With the glitter pen draw very simple snowflakes, distributed evenly over the top of the package. Allow the snowflakes to dry. Draw snowflakes on the sides of the package, allowing each side to dry before decorating the next. Do not draw snowflakes on the bottom of the box.

#43: Christmas

A pocket full of cheer

You will need: gift wrap in a holiday pattern; contrasting ribbon for the bow; several short stems of real or artificial greens; gift card

Fold the paper as shown. Keeping the paper folded, wrap the box, positioning the fold slightly below the center of the box. Tape a length of ribbon around the box just below the fold. Make a Simple Loops Bow (page 31) and glue or tape it to the package. Tuck several stems of greens into the fold. Tuck the gift card behind the greens.

#44: Christmas

Merry holiday stars

You will need: red or green shiny paper sack; self-adhesive star stickers; twist tie; gift wrap ribbon for the bow (red, green or gold or perhaps dotted or gingham apparel ribbon); star-shaped gift tag with a string loop (use pattern from Chapter 4); 4 or 5 pipe cleaners

Apply star stickers to the front and back of the paper sack. Wrap your gift in tissue paper and put it in the sack. Gather the top together and secure with a twist tie. Tie the ribbon in a bow over the twist tie, slipping the loop of the gift tag onto the ribbon before you tie the bow. Press star stickers back to back over one end of each pipe cleaner and tuck the opposite ends firmly into the gathered top. Bend the pipe cleaners slightly to give a jaunty look.

#45: Christmas

Christmas flowers

You will need: holiday paper in a small print, stripe or solid color; satin sheen gift wrap ribbon to wrap around the package; wide satin sheen gift wrap ribbon for the petals of the poinsettias; 3 yellow pompons cut from medium ball fringe

Wrap the box neatly with paper. Wrap ribbon around the box the long way and tape it in back. Make three poinsettias: For each flower, cut six petals (adjusting the size according to the size of the box). Glue the petals together with the points meeting to make the center. Glue a pompon over the center. Glue the flowers to the ribbon on the box.

#46: Christmas

Traditional holly wreath

You will need: holiday gift wrap in a small print or narrow stripe; shiny green paper for the holly leaves; small red pompons from ball fringe or red cinnamon candies (red-hots or imperials) for the berries; 1¼-inch-wide crushable ribbon for the bow

Wrap the box neatly with holiday gift wrap. Using the pattern in Chapter 4, outline and cut out as many holly leaves as you need to make a wreath as shown in the drawing. (The number of leaves depends on the size of the box.) Crease each leaf in half the long way. Arrange the leaves on the package and glue each one down with a dab or two of glue. Glue the pompons or candies in position on the wreath. Make a Crisp Full Bow (page 32) and glue or tape it to the package. To make a tag, cut out one more leaf and write the recipient's name on the white side of the paper. Glue the leaf, white side up, near the bow.

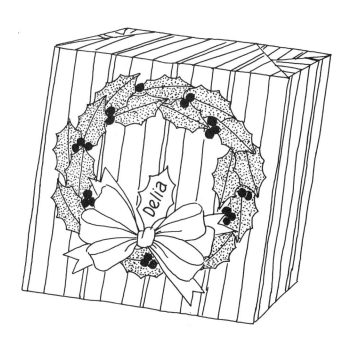

#47: Christmas

Yummy gingerbread house

You will need: kraft paper; 2 gold stretch ties; candy canes, lollipops and small wrapped candies; red cinnamon candies (red-hots or imperials)

This gingerbread house wrapping is fun for a child. Wrap the box neatly in kraft paper. Place the stretch ties around the corners of the box. With a pencil, draw a simple house as shown in the drawing. Glue wrapped candies along the roof lines and across the bottom. Glue candy canes and lollipops on each side of the house and peppermint sticks for the door. (If the sticks are too long, unwrap, break them to the correct size and rewrap, cutting off the excess cellophane.) Glue cinnamon candies on the roof, around the door and to make a window. (The kids can eat the wrapped candies but don't let them munch on the glued cinnamon candies.) Write your message in crayon above the house.

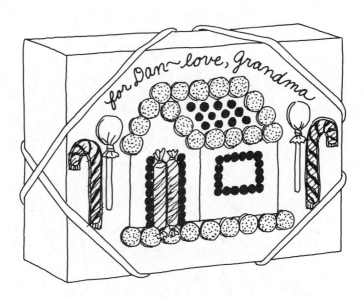

#48: Christmas

Funny felt friend

You will need: bright, solid-color or dotted gift wrap; about 12 small pompons in a color contrasting with the gift wrap; chubby yarn for the border; white felt; bits of ribbon for the scarf; 2 small buttons; a few small white pompons

Wrap the box neatly with the paper. Glue a contrasting pompon near each corner of the top of the box and pieces of chubby yarn between the pompons to make a border. To make the snowman, cut three circles of white felt in graduated sizes and glue them, slightly overlapping, in the center of the box. Add several contrasting pompons to make the hat, some bits of ribbon for the scarf and two buttons on the center circle. Glue a few white pompons around the snowman to represent snowflakes.

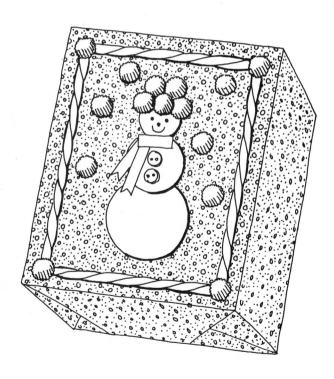

#49: Christmas

Bright golden garland

You will need: holiday gift wrap in a small print, stripe or solid color; gold or silver metallic garland; crushable gift wrap ribbon, 1¼ to 1½ inches wide, in a contrasting color; 6 or 8 small Christmas balls; 5-inch piece of thin wire (florist's wire is easy to work with)

Wrap the box neatly with holiday paper. Glue a piece of garland in a circle on the top of the box. Carefully tie up the box with ribbon, over the garland, and knot without making a bow. Clip off the excess ribbon. String six or eight small balls on the piece of wire and twist the ends of the wire together. Push three or four balls to each end of the wire loop and twist the loop in the middle as shown. Lay the loop of balls over the knot and tape in place. Make a Crisp Full Bow (page 32) and glue it over the knot and the twisted wire. Arrange the balls attractively on both sides of the bow.

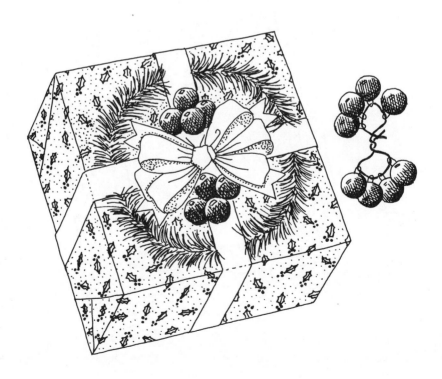

#50: Christmas

Victorian Christmas bouquet

You will need: gold or velvet ribbon about 1 inch wide, depending on the size of the round tin or box; round white or gold doily, slightly smaller than the top of the box; thin wire; 2 or 3 small Christmas balls; 2 or 3 small pinecones; 5 or 6 artificial holly leaves with wires extending from the stems; gift tag or card

This wrapping is for a round tin or box. Cross two pieces of ribbon over the tin and tape securely on the bottom. Glue the doily, centered, to the crossed ribbons. Attach a short piece of wire to each ball and to the bottom of each pinecone. Twist the wires together at the base of the balls, pinecones and holly leaves. Clip off the excess wire and tuck the remaining wire up into the grouping. Arrange the elements attractively, with four of the holly leaves pointing north, south, east and west. Attach the arrangement to the top of the tin by gluing the four holly leaves to the doily. Tuck a gift tag or card under the ribbon and doily. No part of the wrapping is glued directly to the tin; the wrapping may be removed and the tin reused.

CHAPTER 6
Special Gifts:
Odd Shapes and Sizes

This chapter deals with special cases—gifts that have strange shapes, gifts that are too large to wrap, gifts that are represented by pieces of paper, gifts of food and wine. Some of the conventional wrapping techniques can be adapted to these special cases, but often you need as much ingenuity as wrapping paper. Try some of the following suggestions.

Bicycles, tricycles and other small vehicles

Don't try to conceal these gifts under a mountain of gift wrap. It's much better simply to ornament and decorate them so they look festive and exciting.

● Wrap and drape a bike with yards of fluffy metallic Christmas garland or fringed paper garland from the party store.

● Festoon a bicycle with white or multicolored Christmas lights. Do this for any gift-giving occasion, not just Christmas.

● Tie the front end of a sled, wagon or skateboard with ribbon and a bow and pile the rest of Junior's presents on the back end.

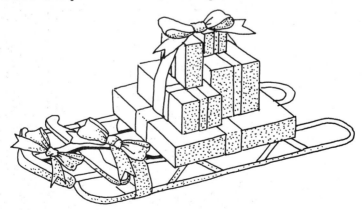

● Weave several colors of crepe paper streamers in the spokes of the wheels. Fasten ribbon streamers to the hand grips and a big bow to the handlebars.

● Tricycles and other small vehicles for toddlers can be set apart in a magic circle of metallic or paper garland and trimmed with a lavish bow on the handlebars or steering wheel.

● Tie or tape lots of bows with long streamers to the hood, sides and handle of a doll carriage.

Sports, games and leisure equipment

Here you are likely to encounter any shape and size from a can of tennis balls to a canoe. The can is easy to deal with (use any cylindrical wrap, for example pages 89 and 91), but you'll have to take a different approach to the canoe: Write a note to the recipient, telling him where the canoe is waiting and any other pertinent information. Add the warranty and whatever brochures you may have collected and put it all in a tissue-lined box. Wrap the box appropriately, tying on a little gift that hints at the contents—perhaps a toy boat or a book on water safety. This is a good way to present any gift that can't actually be handed over—a car, a pony, a complete set of garden furniture, etc.

A lot of sports and games equipment does not come in boxes. When you buy a piece that has no box or container but could fit in one, always ask the store to find one for you. They may happen to have in the stock room a carton that would suit perfectly. This will save you time and trouble. If they can't help you, try to find a box yourself. Line the box with tissue and then wrap, referring to other parts of this book for wrapping ideas.

If you can't unearth a box of the right size, the following guidelines will help with some of the difficulties of wrapping sports equipment.

● Wrap a ball, a hockey mask, a helmet or anything rounded (even a catcher's mitt) in a fabric sack or drawstring bag (pages 50–51). Or put it, wrapped in tissue paper, in a shiny paper shopping bag. Tape the handles together and tie bows over the tape. Use team colors for the ribbons if the gift is for a fan or team player.

● A long, narrow item, like a baseball bat or golf club, can be wrapped in a long narrow piece of wrapping paper.

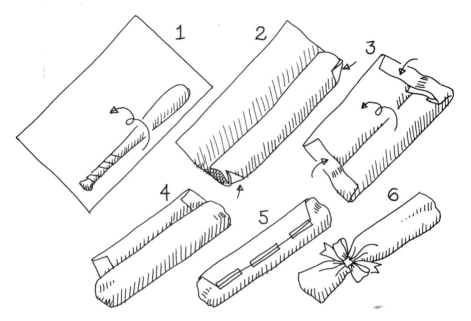

● Slip any kind of racket into a flat paper bag and tie as shown. Decorate the bag.

● Inflatable beach toys and balls should be blown up and then wrapped or tied with ribbon.
● Skis, hockey sticks or an unstrung bow can be spiraled with metallic or paper garlands or with crepe paper streamers.
● Put a group of smaller, related items—weights, a book on weight training, a sweat suit—in a canvas tote, small duffle bag or small backpack.

Refrigerators, lounge chairs and other enormous gifts

These large items break down into two groups, the boxed and the unboxed. There are many ways to present either one.

If the gift is boxed, the first thing to do is paint the box. This is a lot easier than it sounds, if you use a quart of latex paint and a roller. If there is any printing on the box, you'll probably have to give it two coats of paint. When the paint is dry, decorate the box: glue on giant polka dots cut from construction paper, gift wrap or even wallpaper; spell out the recipient's name in giant paper letters; make a blue ribbon medallion from crepe paper and poster board, as shown in the drawing. Glue the medallion to the box and write "MOM" in the center.

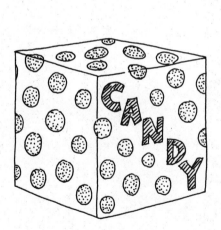

The following ideas will work even if you can't manage to paint the box.

● Tape a bouquet of five or six helium balloons to the top of the box. Add lots of curly paper streamers and let them cascade over the sides. This is a fine presentation for a smaller gift like a sewing machine, typewriter or computer, too.

● Wrap the box horizontally with several colors of crepe paper streamers. Secure the crepe paper with tape loops here and there.

● Cut pieces of gift wrap to fit each side and the top of the box. Attach with spray adhesive.

● Get a roll or two of shelf paper and wrap it around the box to simulate wide ribbon. Make a big bow from a loop of shelf paper fastened in the middle with another loop of shelf paper.

Unboxed gifts need to be dressed up or covered up.

● For Christmas giving, top off an antique dresser, piano, Ping-Pong table or other flat gift with a small evergreen tree decorated with tinsel and lights. Drape swags of pine or boxwood garland over a large gift or hang a ribbon-trimmed wreath on it.

● Most large gifts can be disguised under a pretty tablecloth, sheet or quilt. The trick here is to call everyone's attention to the mysterious object and then whisk off the covering with a flourish.

● You can also hide a gift behind a screen (borrowed if you don't have one in the house), with a little hanging sign saying "MARGARET'S PRESENT." (This only works with adults; kids peek.)

● At any time of the year you can outline a large gift with white or multicolored lights.

Money, checks and other important pieces of paper

The problem with a gift in the form of a piece of paper is that it looks insignificant no matter what it actually represents. For this reason you will want to wrap it in a way that is tasteful yet noticeable. The following ideas are described as wrappings for money or checks, but keep in mind that they can easily be adapted for other pieces of paper like theater or concert tickets, magazine subscriptions, club memberships, hand-lettered poems and gift certificates.

When giving a straightforward gift of money, either check or cash, simple wrapping is better. In fact, the larger the amount the more dignified the wrapping should be. For example, a really impressive check might be enclosed in an envelope with a note written on your personal stationery and then slipped into a handsome leather folder.

Here are some dignified but less formal presentations:

● Make a folder from a sheet of fine artist's paper, enclosing the check as shown below.

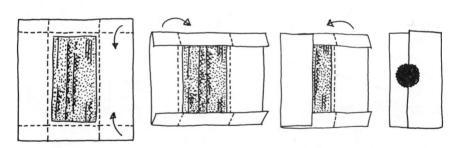

● Fold the check and slip it into a small white envelope. Place the envelope in a bed of crisp but slightly crumpled tissue paper in a clean white box (perhaps a 5-inch cube). Tie the box with ribbon and a bow. An alternative: roll the check up and tie it with a bit of satin ribbon. Nest the roll in the tissue paper and wrap as above. A third possibility: slip the check into an envelope, put it into a flat box (the kind used for gloves or wallets) lined with tissue paper and tie with ribbon.

● Give a beautiful orchid corsage, spring bouquet or a half-dozen tea roses in a florist's box, with the check folded and tucked into the gift card envelope. If you prefer, you can do the same thing using a small, pretty plant like African violets. In all cases, the gift should be delivered by you and not by the florist.

If the gift of money is intended for some specific purpose, try to find a container that suggests that purpose. For example, you might tuck money for a trip in a little toy suitcase. Put a check in a pencil box if it is meant to be used for school fees, in a big aluminum salt-shaker if it is for cooking lessons or rolled up in a miniature dollhouse chest if it is for furniture. Wrap with paper and ribbon and attach a gift tag stating the purpose of the gift.

If there is no specific purpose, find a pretty container like a round, wood, Shaker-style box, a patterned tin or a satin lingerie bag. Line with plenty of tissue paper and put the check in. Wrap the container, referring to the other chapters in this book for suggestions.

Here are two informal ways to present a check:

● Roll up the check and put it in a plastic egg. Nest the egg in a bed of green cellophane grass in a small basket. Tie ribbon to the handle of the basket and attach a gift tag. This is a good wrapping for theater or concert tickets, too.

● Put the check in a 6″ × 9″ envelope along with a piece of shirt cardboard cut slightly smaller than the envelope. Wrap the envelope with paper and ribbon as if it were a package. Use this style of wrapping for gift certificates, with a larger envelope if necessary.

A gift of money to a child calls for a whimsical wrapping.

● Make a money-face from poster board, using coins for eyes and nose and an accordion-folded bill for bow tie or whiskers as shown below. Place the money-face in a tissue-lined box and wrap with paper and ribbon.

● Buy or make a simple kite and tie accordion-folded bills to the tail as shown in the drawing. Be sure to include a ball of string for flying the kite.

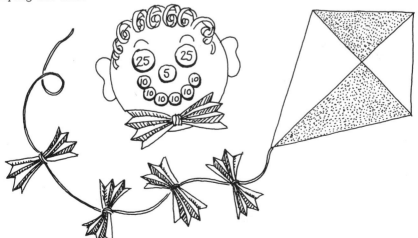

Food and wine

Presentation is extremely important with food and wine because the eyes give the go-ahead to the taste buds. The packaging and the wrapping should be tempting and appetizing. Whether the food is homemade or purchased, tart or sweet, plain or fancy, the better it looks, the more delightful the taste experience. If food is particularly handsome or appealing, choose a presentation that permits the food to show—perhaps a jar or basket. In any case, be sure to pack and carry food and wine so they are protected from both contamination and breakage.

Here are some suggestions for wrapping gifts of food:

● Use a flat foundation like a tray, breadboard or serving plate for this wrapping. It is particularly appropriate for plastic-wrapped foods like bread, fruitcake or coffeecake. Place the wrapped food in the center of the tray and anchor it underneath with tape loops. Tie wide ribbon around the tray using the same tying technique used for packages (page 28) and taping the ribbon on the bottom of the tray if necessary. Make a generous bow.

● The same idea works well with round bowls, baskets or baking tins. For Christmas gifts you can tuck greens or holly under the food or under the ribbon for a festive look.

● Jars are good for holding cookies, candies, nuts, snack mixtures and other small foods, as well as jams, sauces, cheese spreads and vinegars. Place a jar in a fabric sack or drawstring bag (pages 50–51), or if the contents are especially pretty, cover only the lid with the traditional pinked fabric circle, tied with gold cord, yarn or grosgrain ribbon.

● Pile small goodies like candies or cookies into a plastic berry basket. Set the basket on a large square of cellophane. Bring the cellophane up and gather over the goodies. Secure with a twist tie and cover the twist tie with a ribbon and a bow.

● For a group of several small food items, use an oblong or rectangular basket. You may be able to get free mushroom or grape baskets by asking the produce manager at the supermarket or your local greengrocer. Wrap each different food separately, pad the basket with packing straw or green cellophane grass and arrange the small packages on the padding. The packages should rise above the sides of the basket and fit snugly in the basket. Tie with wide ribbon as shown, taping the ribbon on the bottom of the basket if necessary.

● Line a small bucket (metal, plastic or a painter's cardboard one) with full sheets of tissue paper or cellophane. Pack the food in the bucket, cushioning it if necessary. Bring the paper together loosely over the food and secure with a twist tie. Cover the twist tie with ribbon and make a pretty bow. Decorate the bucket with seals or stickers.

● Do the same using a basket instead of a bucket. If the basket has a handle, tie flowers, greens or even autumn leaves to it with a big bow.

● Ask your neighborhood take-out food place if you can buy a few of the little white cardboard boxes they use. Pack your food gift in the box and close it securely. Tie a ribbon around the box as shown and decorate the box with gummed stickers.

● Make small muslin bags with pinked edges (fabric sacks, pages 50–51) to hold coffee beans, candies, pistachio nuts or something exotic like dried mushrooms or dried tomatoes. Tie with gingham ribbon, add a cinnamon stick or two and make a bow.

● Present food in an inexpensive lunch box. Try to get a solid color box and decorate with stickers or seals. Pack the food securely inside, using tissue paper or packing material to keep the food from rattling around. Close tightly and add ribbon bows on the handle.

● Spray-paint a clean coffee tin, fill with cookies or perhaps a dried fruit mixture and top with its plastic lid. Cover the lid with a pinked circle of fabric and tie with narrow ribbon.

● Consider what you have around the house to use for packaging a food gift. Sturdy paper plates, plastic glasses, clean clay or plastic flower pots, a plastic shoe box, paper sacks and shopping bags all make perfectly adequate containers.

● And don't forget the round and square tins that are traditionally used for packing cookies. See page 115 for a great wrap using a round tin.

Wrapping a bottle of wine is a perennial problem because it is such an awkward shape and weight. Try one of these simple, attractive designs.

● Dress up a plain brown bottle bag or shiny colorful bottle bag.

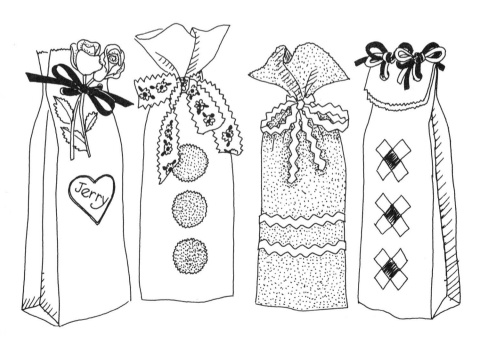

● Put the bottle in a metal bucket and surround it with foam packing bits to keep it propped at an angle. Fill with foam bits only as far as necessary. Pile lots of curly paper streamers (from the party store) over the foam bits and around the handle. Tie ribbon bows to each side of the handle. This works well with a cardboard bucket, too, omitting the ribbon bows if there is no handle. Tie a bow around the neck of the bottle instead.

● Fill a long, narrow basket with packing straw or metallic garland. Place the bottle in the basket, nestle it into the packing material and tie all around the basket with very wide ribbon.